CAPE COD
Nights

CAPE COD Nights

• HISTORIC BARS, CLUBS & DRINKS •

CHRISTOPHER SETTERLUND

AMERICAN PALATE

Published by American Palate
A division of The History Press
Charleston, SC
www.historypress.com

Copyright © 2019 by Christopher Setterlund
All rights reserved

Front cover, top left: courtesy of KingsofCapeCod.com; *top center*: courtesy of Kathy Sullivan Porter; *top right*: courtesy of Sturgis Library; *bottom*: courtesy of Falmouth Historical Society. *Back cover*: courtesy of Cezar Del Valle, TheaterTalks.com; *inset*: courtesy of Sam Howzit.

First published 2019

Manufactured in the United States

ISBN 9781467140058

Library of Congress Control Number: 2019935347

Notice: The information in this book is true and complete to the best of our knowledge. It is offered without guarantee on the part of the author or The History Press. The author and The History Press disclaim all liability in connection with the use of this book.

All rights reserved. No part of this book may be reproduced or transmitted in any form whatsoever without prior written permission from the publisher except in the case of brief quotations embodied in critical articles and reviews.

This book is dedicated with love to my mother, Laurie Sullivan, and my sisters, Katie Setterlund, Lindsay Adams and Ashley Adams, who have been my rocks through tough times and for whom I am so grateful to have in my life. You deserve to be recognized, and I love you all very much.

CONTENTS

Acknowledgements	9
Introduction and Cape Cod's Oldest Tavern	11
1. Atlantic House	13
2. Beachcomber	17
3. Blue Moon Dancing Pavilion	22
4. Bournehurst on the Canal	25
5. Brothers Four	29
6. Cape Cod Coliseum	34
7. Cape Cod Music Circus / Melody Tent	38
8. Casino by the Sea	43
9. Chatham Squire	47
10. The Columns	51
11. Compass Lounge	56
12. Deacon's Perch	60
13. Guido Murphy's	64
14. Higgins Tavern	68
15. Improper Bostonian / Your Father's Mustache	72
16. Joe's Twin Villa	76
17. Johnny Yee's	80
18. Lincoln Lodge	84
19. Mill Hill Club	88
20. Mill Hill Pavilion	93

Contents

21. Old Colony Tap	97
22. On the Rocks	101
23. Panama Club	104
24. Pilgrim Club / Piggy's	108
25. Pufferbellies	112
26. Rainbow Ballroom	117
27. Rick's Outer Bar	121
28. Sandy Pond Club	125
29. Smith's Olde Surrey Room	129
30. Southward Inn	133
31. Storyville	137
32. Velvet Hammer / Red Door / Backside Saloon	141
33. Windjammer	145
34. Zack's Lounge	148
Note	153
Bibliography	155
About the Author	157

ACKNOWLEDGEMENTS

Very special thanks go out to the following people who helped immensely by sharing information, stories, photos and more about many of the historic spots forthcoming. Rebecca Lufkin-Catron (Lincoln Lodge), Brian Braginton-Smith (Sandy Pond Club), Barbara Stone Amidon (Deacon's Perch), Sam Sherman of SamsScrapbook.com (Higgins Tavern), Mary Sicchio and Mavis Robinson of Bourne Historical Society (Bournehurst on the Canal, Blue Moon), David Dunlap of BuildingProvincetown.com (Pilgrim Club, Piggy's, Old Colony Tap, Atlantic House), Peter and David Troutman of Scargo Café, Duncan Oliver of the Historical Society of Yarmouth (Mill Hill Club, Mill Hill Pavilion), Lucy Loomis and the Sturgis Library, Joseph Diggs of JoeDiggsArt.com (Joe's Twin Villa), Mashpee Public Library (On the Rocks, Zack's Place), Meg Costello of Falmouth Museums On the Green (Brothers Four), John Morgan (Pufferbellies), all of the great people in the "You're Really from Barnstable" Facebook group, Dan McCarthy of the Kings of Cape Cod, Johnny Yee, Amy Bourbon of Brewster Historical Society (Woodshed), Rick Weeks (Rick's Outer Bar), Dennis Historical Society, Salvador Vasques of My Provincetown Memorabilia Collection, Dan Murray (Beachcomber) and Diana Batchelor of Pilgrim Monument and Provincetown Museum.

This project would not have been possible without the love and support of my large extended family. In addition to those this book is dedicated to, I would also like to thank my Grampa John Sullivan and his wife of more than seventy years, my Nina Rosemarie Sullivan; my brother, Matt; my nieces

Acknowledgements

and nephews Kaleigh, Emma, Liam, Landon, Lucas and Sylvie; my father, Jack; my uncles Bob, Steve, Eric and John; my aunts Kelly, Emma, Susan and Amy; my cousins Donna, Ryane, Patrick, Sarah, Keith, Tracey and Kathleen; and my Nana in heaven.

I am also forever grateful to a special group of friends I have. The great Bill DeSousa-Mauk, without whom this book would not exist. Steve, DJW, Monique, Mike G., Deanna and Mike, Fitzy and Cape Cloth, Meg, Judy, Dawn, Crystal and Adam, Shayna, Maui, Debbie and the entire Clark family. The Jones family and the Bunker family. I would like to thank Miss Emily Wood for believing in me when I really needed it.

Also a special thank-you to the website Liquor.com for the tremendous cocktail recipes sprinkled throughout this book.

INTRODUCTION AND CAPE COD'S OLDEST TAVERN

We all have to work somewhere, somehow, to make it in the world. Many of us work long hours, possibly filled with stress from the job. When those long days are done, people need to find ways to unwind and recover. For centuries, there have been many popular ways that the workforce chose to fill those hours away from work.

Barrooms, saloons, pubs, taverns or bars—whatever they may be called, places to unwind after a tough day at work or to meet up with one's mates—have been a staple of life in America since its inception in the fifteenth century. The oldest tavern in the country, White Horse Tavern, located in Newport, Rhode Island, was opened in 1673.

The oldest tavern on Cape Cod was located on Great Island in present-day Wellfleet. Owned by Samuel Smith, the tavern operated during the period approximately between 1690 and 1740. The tavern became a popular spot for fishermen pursuing their catches of whales, oysters or other sea life. In the days when Great Island was not a peninsula, whalers would row their way over and enjoy drinks such as a toddy (made with bourbon, honey and fresh lemon juice) or a flip (beer, rum and sugar). The tavern site had been lost to history for more than two centuries, becoming more of a legend among the hills of Great Island. In 1969, the site was rediscovered and excavated, with many exciting artifacts being found and moved to the Salt Pond Visitors Center in Eastham. Today, one can visit the site and see the remains of its stone foundation.

Introduction and Cape Cod's Oldest Tavern

However, places to unwind after dark have not been limited to bars. Nightclubs, discos, juke joints, honky-tonks, social halls and more have been terms used for a place to include some dancing with your drinks. Their roots trace back to 1886, when Webster Hall in Manhattan opened and was referred to as a "social club."

On Cape Cod, nightlife has grown and evolved over the years. It has gone from the days before electricity, when whiskey and bourbon were slung, to today's modern mixed drinks. It has gone from moving-picture shows and barn dances to happy hours and DJs. It has gone from many clubs having in-house orchestras to most establishments having some sort of digital music platform. There was a peak, a golden age, which will be referenced many times in the pages to come. From the late 1960s through the mid-1980s, the nightlife on Cape Cod brought people from Boston to New York City and all over New England. It was a time looked back on fondly, the likes of which will probably never be seen again.

Times have changed significantly; however, the one thing that has stayed the same is the desire to have fun. Americans on the whole work too much: a 2016 Bureau of Labor study showed that adults aged twenty-five to fifty-four worked an average of 42.8 hours per week. Today as much as ever, people need a break from the daily grind. A favorite bar or nightclub can provide such a stress release.

In the pages ahead we will look back into Cape Cod history to share the stories of some of the most legendary nightlife locations to have ever graced the shores of this peninsula. Some still exist to this day, some have been replaced by others in the same location and others have been lost to history. Put on your favorite vinyl album, eight-track, cassette tape, CD, mp3 or streamed playlist, kick your feet up with a favorite drink or mix one from the forthcoming pages and enjoy the historic nightlife of Cape Cod.

1.
ATLANTIC HOUSE

4/6 Masonic Place, Provincetown
1798–present

There are very few places on Cape Cod that are considered both historic and contemporary. The Atlantic House, or A-House, is one of those rarities. After more than two centuries in operation, it is still going strong, despite undergoing changes along the way to keep up with the times.

Before being christened the Atlantic House in 1871, the building on Masonic Place in Provincetown had already lived a pair of lives in history. The first incarnation of the building was Pease's Tavern, constructed by Edgartown resident Daniel Pease in 1798. Pease would gain notoriety when he was named Provincetown's first postmaster on January 1, 1801. The tavern would be run under his watchful eye for more than three decades before his death in 1834 from cholera while traveling on a ship from New York.

After Pease's death, his tavern would be purchased by Benjamin Allstrum and fittingly renamed the Allstrum House. Allstrum had made money selling supplies to ships and also in real estate, and he was looking for new investment opportunities. In the nearly forty years that he owned it, the building would see time as a courthouse and the last stop of the stagecoach connecting Orleans and Provincetown. With the availability of railroad travel, the stagecoach became less relevant, and Allstrum would sell the building to a young Portuguese sailor named Frank Potter Smith in late 1871. Allstrum died in 1874 at age forty-nine. Smith, however, would change the course of the building forever.

The present-day Atlantic House. *Courtesy of Salvador R. Vasques III Collection, Pilgrim Monument and Provincetown Museum Collection.*

It was Smith who changed the building's name to the Atlantic House, beginning the tradition that continues to this day. He ran the building as a clean and welcoming tavern, restaurant and hotel, attracting visitors and locals alike. It prided itself on being a place where visitors could get meals at all hours. Smith would regale visitors with his tales of the sea, only adding to his genial manner and big-hearted hospitality. He held on to the reins of the Atlantic House for forty-five years until selling it to the Iris family, specifically Ira G. Iris, in September 1916 and retiring.

Iris oversaw some of the Atlantic House's most formidable years. In 1917 and 1918, famed playwright Eugene O'Neill stayed at the hostel, and there is even a plaque commemorating that he wrote his plays *Ile*, *Moon of the Caribbees*, *The Long Voyage Home* and *In the Zone* while staying there. Iris also gave Atlantic House the distinction of being home to America's very last town crier, Walter Smith, who worked for the establishment until shortly before his death in 1932.

As the Great Depression gripped the country, the already iconic Atlantic House continued to find new ways to bring in locals and visitors. If one did not like the dollar chicken or lobster dinners, perhaps they'd enjoy staying in one of the thirty-five rooms. However, Iris upped the game by adding cabaret shows to their spectacular parties and spacious dance floor. This would lead to an expansion of the building, a revamping of the dining area and, most ambitious, the renovation of the nearby Small House to become the Atlantic House Tourist Home in 1938. It all nearly came crashing down though. In April 1939, a defective oil stove exploded soon after being lit, causing a fire that resulted in $15,000 worth of damage ($272,000 in 2018). Repairs were quick, and in less than three weeks the legendary nightspot was back in business.

In 1949, Atlantic House changed hands again as Reggie Cabral took over along with his brother-in-law Frank Hurst. It was at this point in time that the decor and entertainment aspects of the business became the focal points. The Cabaret Room hosted summertime revues starring impresario Julius Monk and costarring Imogene Coca. The 1950s saw Eartha Kitt, Billie Holiday and Ella Fitzgerald among others perform there. There was also the night that jazz singer Stella Brooks performed a song with impromptu lyrics written on the spot by Tennessee Williams. The Big Room, born in 1960, would soon house more amazing jazz performance from legends such as Miles Davis.

It was in the 1970s that Cabral and the Atlantic House made it a point to appeal to the growing gay community in Provincetown. Though it had been gay-friendly since the 1950s, beginning in 1976, the upstairs Carriage Room was renamed the Macho Room, the Tap Room became the Little Bar (perfect for locals) and the jazzy Big Room became the Dance Club. As the twentieth century ended, the Atlantic House had truly become a perfect mix of the two sides of Provincetown's history coin: the fishing village and the gay-friendly small town.

Today, the Cabral family is still running the Atlantic House, which celebrated its 230th year in existence in 2018 with Reggie's daughter April Cabral-Pitzner heading the ship. It maintains the rustic nautical feel of the original 1798 Pease's Tavern while keeping a foot in the present with state-of-the-art lighting and sound. Now mainly referred to as the A-House, this iconic nightspot shows no signs of falling behind the times. With a great atmosphere, loyal clientele, tremendous location and tremendous ownership, it seems clear the A-House will be around at the turn of the next century, as well.

A visitor to the Atlantic House during the jazzy heyday of the 1950s may have enjoyed a popular mixed concoction called a Sea Breeze.

Sea Breeze

1 ½ ounces vodka
4 ounces fresh grapefruit juice
1 ½ ounces cranberry juice
1 lime wedge

Preparation: Pour everything into a highball glass, stir and decorate with a lime wedge. For a foamy finish, shake in cocktail mixer.

2.
BEACHCOMBER

1120 Cahoon Hollow Road, Wellfleet
1953–present

Cape Cod is home to 559.6 miles of coastline. Much of that is pristine beach used by residents and visitors alike. It is also home to hundreds of restaurants and bars. There are a good number of waterfront establishments. But few, if any, have combined the beautiful scenery of the beach with a quality and unique atmosphere as has the Beachcomber in Wellfleet.

The story of the Beachcomber as an establishment goes back more than sixty years and is still going strong today. The history of the building that houses the Beachcomber goes back even farther. The Beachcomber's home was originally a lifesaving station located at Cahoon Hollow Beach. It was one of nine such stations built along the Outer Cape in 1897 due to the unfortunate frequency of shipwrecks in the area. The other stations were built at Race Point in Provincetown; Highlands, Peaked Hill Bars and Pamet in Truro; Nauset in Eastham; Orleans; and Chatham and Monomoy in Chatham.

In July 1946, three of the stations, including the station at Cahoon Hollow, were deactivated. The station remained unoccupied for seven years until it gained a second life far from its original purpose. In 1953, Russell Gallagher, who had summered in Wellfleet and Cahoon Hollow Beach as a child, along with his wife, Ruth, purchased the vacant building and rechristened it the Wellfleet Beachcomber's Club. In keeping with the name of the new

Cape Cod Nights

An aerial view of the Beachcomber. *Courtesy of Dan Murray/The Beachcomber.*

establishment, Gallagher filled one of the rooms of the building with items procured from the sands below through actual beachcombing. In 1955, Gallagher also took a job working for Ocean Spray, a career that would last twenty-three years.

In 1958, the fledgling establishment received the town's first club license and was referred to as a cocktail lounge and snack bar. It would dodge a major bullet a few years later. In August 1961, President John F. Kennedy would sign a bill creating the Cape Cod National Seashore. The park would encompass 43,607 acres, including the land on which the Beachcomber stood. But luckily, because of the "grandfather clause," the privately owned business was allowed to remain open despite residing inside a national park.

Though fairly successful (and benefiting from a view that could not be beat), the initial years of the Beachcomber were only the tip of the iceberg. Gallagher remained in charge of the waterfront establishment for twenty-five years before selling it to Todd LeBart—who had previously been part of a group that had run the nearby Duck Creek Tavern—and Hugh Dunbar in May 1978. It was after this sale that the old lifesaving station became one of the preeminent nightspots on Cape Cod.

Historic Bars, Clubs & Drinks

The interior of the Beachcomber.
Courtesy of Olde Towne Floors, Wellfleet.

The new owners fought hard and were granted a year-round liquor license to remain in operation on weekends in the off-season, changed from a seasonal license that Gallagher had operated under. They also embraced the trends of the times by referring to their spot as a "disco in the dunes" in local advertisements. Those coming to the club to dance became the entertainment in the days before live music would take center stage.

Within two years, despite the year-round liquor license being changed back to a seasonal license after problems arose during the off-season in 1979, LeBart and Dunbar acquiesced to the town and changed their license after a threat of potential revocation of their commercial certification with the Cape Cod National Seashore. The change was made and crisis averted. As the 1980s progressed, LeBart and Dunbar made more changes that would reward them handsomely after struggling to get by in their early years as owners.

The 'Comber began to push live music over the DJ booths of the late 1970s. Local acts like the Incredible Casuals and the Cyclones made the establishment part of their schedule, bringing in crowds and easily filling the building to its maximum capacity of 260. In the days since, the list of musical acts that have graced the stage at the Beachcomber is wide-ranging, touching nearly every musical genre imaginable. From more local legends like Bim Skala Bim to reggae originators Toots and the Maytals, alternative rockers They Might Be Giants, big-name bands like NRBQ and jazz saxophonist Maceo Parker, to a special unannounced show by Weezer in 2001, the stage has showcased some impressive talent.

LeBart and Dunbar knew they needed a signature drink to go along with the ocean views and amazing live music. They would find such a drink in a little ditty they call the Goombay Smash. Though the exact recipe is kept under wraps, it is described as containing amber rum, coconut rum, apricot brandy, orange juice, pineapple juice and a Myers float. As of 2018, more than three million of these have been sold at the 'Comber.

The music, drinks, views and camaraderie made the opening each season of the Beachcomber a ritual for locals and visitors alike that only grew as the 1980s entered the 1990s. The establishment evolved from a more traditional surf bar to a place where everyone went to dance and be seen. Now after more than sixty years as an eating and drinking establishment—forty under the current regime—the Beachcomber is an icon. It still boasts a full lunch and dinner menu to accompany its live music and unparalleled ocean views.

The only thing that might threaten the success of the 'Comber is Mother Nature. During the summer of 2017, a prolonged heavy rainstorm caused the collapse of part of the establishment's parking lot, including a car falling into the sinkhole. Despite this, the iconic 'Comber is still going strong as of 2018 and will no doubt have continued success for years to come.

Though the exact details of the Goombay Smash are kept under wraps, if one was to have visited the Beachcomber in the 1990s, as its seasonal opening became a Cape Cod ritual, one could have sampled another drink that entered its prime at the same time, the Long Island Iced Tea.

Long Island Iced Tea

¾ ounce gin
¾ ounce white rum
¾ ounce silver tequila
¾ ounce vodka

¾ ounce triple sec
¾ ounce simple syrup
¾ ounce lemon juice
cola

Preparation: Fill a highball or hurricane glass with ice and add all of the ingredients except the cola. Top with a splash of cola, stir briefly and garnish with a lemon wedge.

3.
BLUE MOON DANCING PAVILION

230 Main Street, Buzzards Bay
1931–mid-1960s

The Cape Cod Canal was opened in 1914 and became a very important waterway, shortening the distance boats had to travel between Boston and cities like New York by roughly 135 miles. The seven-mile-long man-made river would create an artificial border between the towns of Bourne and Buzzards Bay, as well as between Sandwich and Sagamore. The parcels of land on either side of the new canal became waterfront and very sought after. It was on one of these parcels on the north side of the canal that a unique piece of Cape Cod nightlife would be created. It was part indoors, part outdoors, yet it was all Blue Moon.

The Blue Moon of Buzzards Bay began as the brainchild of George Hubbard Blakeslee. A professor of history and international relations at Clark University in Worcester, Massachusetts, Blakeslee regularly summered in the Bourne / Buzzards Bay area. The professor's summer home on Electric Avenue in Buzzards Bay once belonged to vaunted actor Joseph Jefferson.

Blakeslee had the idea to create a perfect feast for the senses—an outdoor dancing pavilion mixing music with the sights of the passing vessels on the canal along with the scents of beautiful summer evenings. The new nightspot would be positioned on a larger parcel of land stretching from Main Street all the way back to the canal. The parking lot would be large enough to fit hundreds of vehicles. It was a recipe for success, and the new venture would be called the Blue Moon.

The Blue Moon opened for business during the Fourth of July week in 1931 and was immediately a huge hit due to its unusual setup. Called anything from a "dancing pavilion" to a "summer dance garden," the new establishment enticed passersby with a blue neon sign along with bright red, yellow and blue lights surrounding the dance floor. Accompanied by the swinging sounds of the orchestra, the kaleidoscope of lights and music called to motorists on Main Street.

Adorned with strings of blue lights stretching from the half moon–shaped stage all the way across the dance floor, it was difficult to miss the Blue Moon. The orchestra played from the stage while throngs of people danced on the floor, which had been made of a special composition and coated with wax so that inclement weather would not damage it. Even those who were not the dancing type could get there early and park their automobile close enough to hear the music from their vehicle. There was even an outdoor garden where folks could sit and enjoy the scenery with the orchestra as the soundtrack. If snacks were so desired, there was a small restaurant tearoom at the entrance to the indoor part of the pavilion. It carried sandwiches, lobster rolls, homemade pastries, refreshments, ice cream and more for the crowds. Blue Moon was open during daylight hours as well, allowing those who were not night owls to enjoy outdoor dancing.

The first season at the Blue Moon was a rousing success. When it came time to reopen in June 1932, the word was out. New entertainment was added to the itinerary, including the popular Midnight Frolics later in the 1930s. These began promptly at 12:01 a.m. on Monday, as alcohol sales were prohibited on Sundays. After adding another successful chapter to his legacy, George Blakeslee decided it was time to move into retirement.

His successor at the Blue Moon came in the form of Philip Lowe. Lowe and his family had summered in neighboring Wareham for decades, and he had routinely patronized the Blue Moon. In 1939, Philip took over Blue Moon and continued its success. As the 1940s passed, Lowe added simple pleasures like table tennis while also routinely employing famed regional musicians the Chick Hathaway Orchestra to grace the pavilion stage.

Lowe sold the Blue Moon property in 1952, but he would have a hand in helping to create the Cod Drive-In Theatre located in the Teaticket village of Falmouth in 1955. Eventually, the establishment would fall into the hands of Bourne resident and young aspiring politician Alex Byron. In 1957, Byron began pushing forward with plans to create an outdoor summer theater along the canal on the eighteen-acre tract of land. The Buzzards Bay Summer Theatre would be a theater in the round and seat between seven hundred and one thousand people and become the focus of the property. This meant that, although the Blue Moon remained open, it became more of a complement to the theater.

The theater did not last very long, with Byron returning his focus to the Blue Moon. He and his family eventually changed the Blue Moon's name to Byron's Landing in the mid-1960s and operated it as a family restaurant until 1986. As of 2018, the original building for the Blue Moon still stands and is home to Buzzards Bay Veterinary Associates.

If one visited the Blue Moon Dancing Pavilion for one of its Midnight Frolics during the heyday of the late 1930s, they may have enjoyed a drink called an Aviation.

Aviation

2 ounces gin
½ ounce Maraschino liqueur
¼ ounce Crème de Violette or Crème Yvette
¾ ounce lemon juice

Preparation: Add all of the ingredients to a shaker and fill with ice. Shake and strain into a cocktail glass. Garnish with a brandied cherry.

4.
BOURNEHURST ON THE CANAL

320 MAIN STREET, BUZZARDS BAY
1920–1933

The Roaring Twenties was a period of tremendous prosperity and good feelings in the United States. It was a time of social and political changes, with Americans leaving farms to move to cities. Jazz, commercial radio stations, motion picture theaters, "flappers," Prohibition and more defined a decade still fondly remembered to this day. On Cape Cod, along the new canal, a spot opened up that captured the good feelings of the Roaring Twenties. It was known simply as the Bournehurst on the Canal, and it would leave a tremendous imprint on Cape Cod in less than a decade and a half.

The Bournehurst began as an idea of Dartmouth, Massachusetts resident Walter Burrows. In January 1920, he purchased two acres of cleared land from the estate of Cyrenius Eldridge, a whaler and section master of the Old Colony Railroad, for $500. Along with partner Ralph Morris, Burrows petitioned the Town of Bourne the following month for the creation of a spot he called the Bournehurst Amusement Company. The project, to be built of fireproof cement and costing approximately $100,000 ($1.3 million in 2018), was nearly unanimously approved by selectmen and townsfolk alike. It was to be constructed as soon as the ground thawed.

Bournehurst would be situated on the north side of the Cape Cod Canal, across the water in Buzzards Bay just south of the present-day CVS at the meeting of Route 28 and Head of the Bay Road. The beautiful scenery would be incorporated into the creation of the building, with

Postcard of Bournehurst on the Canal. *Courtesy of Cezar Del Valle, TheatreTalks.com.*

windows allowing the viewing of vessels passing by only a few hundred feet south. The simple exterior would house a more attractive interior with an old rose-and-white color scheme, French gray light fixtures, private boxes for parties and room for up to 1,500 on the largest dance floor in southeastern Massachusetts. The passing of the Eighteenth Amendment, creating Prohibition in January 1919, meant that any new endeavor such as the Bournehurst needed to be good, clean fun, not reliant on booze. It would be just that.

Despite the building not being fully completed, a huge gala was put together for early that summer. Opening night for the newly christened Bournehurst on the Canal was Saturday, July 10, 1920. It was a stunning success, with 2,100 tickets sold for the event and $250 made from the sales of ice cream and cigars alone. Bournehurst continued to hold weekend events until construction of the moving-picture theater and restaurant was completed on July 31. Things did get off to a rocky start; during one of the initial evening dances, a storm knocked out power, causing people to have to wait several hours for electricity to be restored. But they made the best of it, as kerosene lanterns were used in the interim.

Bournehurst retained much of its crowds even after tourists departed following Labor Day weekend. Dances with the live orchestra, food and motion pictures meant this hot spot had something for everyone. Walter

Burrows escaped injury after a serious car accident in March 1921 and soon thereafter began stepping up his efforts at his already beloved establishment. This included a Midnite Frolic dance held on July 4 from 12:00 a.m. to 3:00 a.m. The overnight romp drew more than 1,500 to the Bournehurst. Burrows brought in one of Leo Reisman's orchestras from Boston's Hotel Brunswick while also hiring famed novelty dance promoter George Pirrie that summer to perform there while he also split time with Mill Hill Pavilion in West Yarmouth. The summer peaked on August 22 with a dance that saw more than 2,200 in attendance.

Burrows would add amateur basketball games and boxing matches to the itinerary in subsequent years. The Bournehurst became a fixture in the community by holding barn dances, school proms and free movies for children called "photo plays." A popular lunchroom opened in 1922, managed by Fred Lutz. It became known for its Sunday clambakes. The exterior grounds were improved in 1924 with trees and shrubs along with a new road to the parking lot that was much safer for automobiles. It had truly become a one-stop spot for all things entertainment for all ages.

As the Roaring Twenties continued, the Bournehurst became a regular stop for up-and-coming artists in the burgeoning jazz scene, including the bands of Duke Ellington, Paul Whiteman, Cab Calloway and others. However, much like the looming stock market crash of 1929, the good times would not last.

On February 15, 1929, Bournehurst was foreclosed on after Walter Burrows had fallen into debt and owed $17,000 ($250,000 in 2018) on the property's mortgage. It was sold at auction to Samuel Resnik of Boston, who paid the property's debt and promised to keep the Bournehurst running and to open it in time for summer.

Though Resnik would sell Bournehurst less than a year later to Charles Schribman, the establishment's success would continue. Managed by Oscar Whipple, the dance pavilion saw perhaps its biggest crowd on July 26, 1930, when Rudy Vallee and his orchestra came to play. The building was filled beyond capacity, with hundreds more waiting outside just to catch a glimpse of the legendary original teen idol pop star. Despite state police being called in, it was nearly impossible to maintain order. This proved to be the last hurrah for the Bournehurst.

Three years after one of the biggest names in entertainment had graced its interior, the Bournehurst was nearly destroyed by a fire. On October 18, 1933, the legendary ballroom burned in what was described as the hottest fire witnesses had ever seen. Ten months later, another fire finished the property off by destroying the theater. Both fires were believed to be deliberate; the total loss of the property was approximately $140,000 ($2.6 million in 2018). The loss of the beloved dance pavilion was immediate for those who frequented it, yet it was also sad to think of what might have been. First, the new rotary in Buzzards Bay, which opened shortly after the construction of the new Bourne Bridge in 1933, was located directly in front of where the Bournehurst had stood. Perhaps it would have enticed passing motorists to stop in. Second, only two months after the first fire, Prohibition was repealed, leaving one to wonder what the inclusion of alcohol sales would have meant for the Bournehurst.

Unfortunately, it is all hypothetical. The Bournehurst on the Canal thrilled thousands in its short thirteen-year history. It was one of the godfathers of Cape Cod nightlife. As of 2018, the spot once housing this icon is occupied by Tamarack Technologies.

If the Bournehurst had remained, perhaps it would have held a Midnite Frolic the night Prohibition was repealed. If so, one could have partaken in a Southside Fizz, the preferred drink of Chicago mobster Al Capone.

Southside Fizz

1 ¼ ounces gin
½ ounce lime juice
½ ounce simple syrup
1 sprig mint
club soda

Preparation: In a shaker, muddle the mint, lime juice and simple syrup. Add the gin and fill with ice. Shake, and strain into a highball glass filled with crushed ice. Stir until frost appears on the outside of the glass. Fill with club soda and garnish with another mint sprig.

5.
BROTHERS FOUR

263 Grand Avenue, Falmouth
1971–1987

Synonymous with the Falmouth Road Race and its creator, Tommy Leonard, this location carved a spectacular legacy in Falmouth Heights. The story of this legendary watering hole actually got its start three thousand miles away in Las Vegas, Nevada, and luck at a game of blackjack.

The four brothers who would make up the name of the establishment were the Robbat brothers, George, Russell, Steven and Alan, all of whom were born in Arlington, Massachusetts. The family patriarch, George Sr., had owned the Jumbo Lounge in Somerville, so the nightlife industry was in the blood of the brothers.

George developed an interest in learning how to win at blackjack after his father had taken the boys on a few trips to Las Vegas. He would learn how to count cards fairly well, enough that casinos caught on and would throw him out. During a successful trip that included Las Vegas and Lake Tahoe, George won big, and that money was used to start a string of successful establishments in New England.

In 1971, George purchased the Terrace Gables Hotel on Grand Avenue in Falmouth Heights. The Terrace Gables, once a posh resort hotel, had been struggling. Despite being in business for more than seventy-five years by that point, it had begun to trend downward during the mid-1950s when the older generation that had frequented the hotel began to pass on. Several prior attempts were made to breathe new life into the property.

The finish line of the 1975 Falmouth Road Race, facing Brothers Four. *Courtesy of Hugo Poisson.*

A small cocktail lounge was created, and the outdoor porch was enclosed to allow for more space. The cocktail lounge was called Club 46—from the hours of 4:00 p.m. to 6:00 p.m., every drink cost forty-six cents. In 1961, the first-floor guest rooms were removed, Club 46 was closed and the enlarged space, to be known as the Frolic Room, opened in July 1961. In 1969, a parking lot was built to help ease the congestion brought about by the new and popular establishment. The younger crowd descended on Falmouth Heights.

In 1971, George and his three brothers renamed the property the Brothers 4 bar. The establishment lay claim to being the Cape's largest entertainment complex with three different clubs under one roof. It was an immediate hit, spawning a pair of sister bars in Somerville and Nashua, New Hampshire.

It was during its infancy that bartender Tommy Leonard, who was also an avid runner, created an iconic event from an average run. Leonard's now famous route began at the Captain Kidd Restaurant on Water Street in Woods Hole and meandered through the town of Falmouth before ending

7.1 miles later in the shadow of the Brothers 4, where Leonard worked. The next year, the first Falmouth Road Race was held, forever cementing the Brothers 4 in the annals of history. The race began with a mere ninety-two participants; as of 2017, it sees more than eleven thousand runners annually.

The Cape's self-proclaimed "largest entertainment complex" was home to many unique and beloved traditions. One popular event was the Beat the Clock Happy Hour, when drinks began as a mere twenty-five cents before jumping to fifty after a period of time, and so on. In addition to this event, the establishment hosted giant weekend pool parties with

The finish line of the Falmouth Road Race facing British Beer Company, which stands near where Brothers Four once did. *Courtesy of Christopher Setterlund.*

barbecues included. Battle of the Sexes, Gong Show, Hot Legs contests, tanning contests—Brothers 4 had seemingly something different every day during its summers in business. The bar routinely had crowds in the hundreds, with some holidays approaching one thousand people inside and on the beach.

However, the popularity of the establishment led to problems with the Falmouth Heights neighborhood. In 1976, the Robbats were taken to court. The neighborhood group claimed that due to the fact that Brothers 4 was not using the property for its original intended use—a resort hotel—it should be forced to adhere to local zoning laws. Despite the fact that the property in fact still did rent out rooms and was grandfathered in the neighborhood, seemingly making it exempt from zoning laws, the court battle continued for more than six years. It was claimed that the Disco Room, Game Room and Pub were too loud and should be closed down. The court case delayed improvements to the property George Robbat wished to make. Despite the efforts Robbat made that actually lessened the noise compared to in the 1960s, the town was unrelenting.

By 1982, Robbat was beginning to acquiesce to the town, changing the interior of the building to merge the three clubs into one. He also began trying to encourage more food sales and other ideas to improve the bar's image. This would include creating a separate entity under the roof known as Yesterdays, keeping up the legacy of the property as a resort hotel. Try as he might, the writing was on the wall. Robbat kept Brothers 4 up and running for a few more years, but pressure from the locals in Falmouth Heights eventually won out. In 1987, the onetime largest entertainment complex on Cape Cod was torn down. Today, the property is occupied by condos.

Despite it being closed for more than three decades, Brothers 4's legacy carries on to this day. Its name is uttered every year when the Falmouth Road Race takes place. It also lives on in the hearts and minds of all of the thousands who frequented it as patrons or employees. In that way, George Robbat succeeded in creating a lasting impression with his revival of the old Terrace Gables resort hotel.

If one visited the Brothers 4 during its heyday in the late 1970s, perhaps he or she would have ordered a Rob Roy.

Rob Roy

2 ounces scotch
¾ ounce sweet vermouth
3 dashes Angostura bitters

Preparation: Add all of the ingredients into a mixing glass over ice and stir. Strain into a chilled cocktail glass. Garnish with 2 speared brandied cherries.

6.
CAPE COD COLISEUM

225 WHITES PATH, SOUTH YARMOUTH
1972–1984

When it comes to historic nightlife, the hot spots do not end with bars and nightclubs. For a little over a decade, there was a place located in a quiet section of South Yarmouth that had entertainment quality unsurpassed on Cape Cod. That place was the Cape Cod Coliseum, and its legend is still strong today.

The Cape Cod Coliseum opened in September 1972. It was a 46,000-square-foot concrete arena that sat between five thousand and six thousand people and cost $1.5 million to build. It was originally owned by Yarmouth real estate agent William Harrison and his partners Gordon Daggett and Bob Kendrick. Harrison eventually bought them out to run it alone. The Coliseum was managed by Richard "Bud" Terrio, initially making waves as a location for ice hockey, both youth and amateur.

Terrio gained notoriety as the man who helped create the Cape Cod Cubs. The Cubs debuted in the Eastern Hockey League in time for the 1972–73 season, with Terrio serving as the team's first president. Many local youth hockey organizations were encouraged to sign up for ice time, filling out much of the Coliseum's schedule during its first season in business.

The first event at the Coliseum was a game between the Boston Braves and Rhode Island Reds of the American Hockey League on September 27, 1972. The Braves were the affiliate of the NHL's Boston Bruins, while the Reds were the affiliate of the New York Rangers.

The Cape Cod Coliseum in the late 1970s. *Courtesy of Todd Kennelly.*

The next spring, the Coliseum began attracting musical entertainment. It was converted into an auditorium capable of holding 6,500 people when the Boston Pops paid a visit in April 1973. So anticipated was this performance that traffic was backed up all the way from the Coliseum entrance to the off-ramps of the Mid-Cape Highway one mile away, not to mention eyewitness accounts of people parking along the highway and scaling the fence to see the show as well.

In the 1970s, some of the biggest names in music graced the stage inside the concrete cube. Artists such as ZZ Top, KISS, Foreigner, Styx, Black Sabbath, Van Halen, Grateful Dead, Heart, Rush and Santana traveled to the little village of South Yarmouth to play for ravenous fans at the Coliseum. As successful as the arena was, turmoil was just below the surface.

Early in 1974, the Coliseum was put up for sale at a value of $2.5 million. The Cape Cod Cubs were not doing well, drawing an average of 2,000 to 2,800 fans per game when the arena could hold just over 5,000 for hockey. In February 1975, the building actually closed for twenty-four hours. A permanent closure was averted when an agreement was made with Bass River Savings Bank to keep operations going. This was in large part due to support from the community and youth hockey.

The Cubs were rechristened the Cape Codders for the 1974–75 season. The writing was on the wall, though. Despite efforts to raise the funds needed to save it, the team folded in 1977. The year before, original owner William Harrison had filed for bankruptcy. The arena was then bought by Ed Fruean.

Fruean owned the Coliseum for three years before its most well-known owner took over. Vince McMahon, the owner of World Wrestling Entertainment, agreed to take over the mortgage payments for the Coliseum from Ed Fruean, using the profits from events run there to pay it. Ironically, it was in the Coliseum offices that McMahon's ascent to the worldwide leader in sports entertainment began. He changed the regional World Wide Wrestling Federation (WWWF) to the World Wrestling Federation (WWF) and created Titan Sports in South Yarmouth.

Wrestling events had been a staple of the Cape Cod Coliseum since the beginning, with stars like Hulk Hogan, Andre the Giant, Bob Backlund, Sgt. Slaughter and others entertaining fans inside the concrete walls. In addition to wrestling, concerts and hockey were also held at the Coliseum. Other events included roller derby, Sesame Street Live On-Ice and a visit from the Boston Lobsters. The latter was a World Team Tennis team led by Wimbledon champion Martina Navratilova and owned by a young Robert Kraft.

The Cape Cod Coliseum continued to bring in big-time acts as the 1980s rolled around. Aerosmith, Def Leppard, The Clash, Talking Heads and Iron Maiden plied their trade with up-and-coming artists inside the arena. While concerts, hockey and other events did well, Vince McMahon's WWF took pro wrestling to an entirely new level. His interest in running the Coliseum waned. McMahon sold the building in 1984 to Christmas Tree Shops, which turned it into a warehouse. Fittingly, the final event held at the Cape Cod Coliseum was a World Wrestling Federation card on June 4, 1984, with Sgt. Slaughter being the final person to entertain people inside its walls.

In the three decades since its closing, the Cape Cod Coliseum has become a footnote in history. The Melody Tent has continued uninterrupted success, bringing in famous acts during the summer. When one passes by the former Coliseum, the outline of its name is still visible on the façade. Otherwise, all that remains of this brilliant flash of light are the memories held dear by so many longtime Cape Codders.

Those who frequented the Cape Cod Coliseum in its heyday may have chosen to drink a frosty Miller Lite. If beer was not the choice, perhaps sipping on a Harvey Wallbanger would suffice to go along with the banging on the drums in the Coliseum.

Harvey Wallbanger

1 ¼ ounces vodka
3 ounces orange juice
½ ounce Galliano L'Autentico (a vanilla-sweet Italian liqueur)

Preparation: Mix vodka and orange juice in a tall glass, float Galliano on top and garnish with an orange slice.

7.
CAPE COD MUSIC CIRCUS / MELODY TENT

21 West Main Street, Hyannis
1950–present

When it comes to nightlife and the entertainment factor that comes along with it, no location on Cape Cod can match the list of talent that has passed under the flaps of the Cape Cod Melody Tent. For more than six decades, it has been wowing audiences throughout the summer. The well-known acts, intimate seating and summer air have made it a destination for visitors and locals alike. In the beginning, though, the Melody Tent's list of performers and shows looked far different from the musicians, comedians and others in the present day.

The concept of an open-air entertainment complex began in 1948 in Lambertville, New Jersey, and was the brainchild of St. John Terrell. Broadway actress Gertrude Lawrence was vacationing in southern Florida when she happened upon a circus tent where actors were performing. It was a modern take on the theater-in-the-round established in Ancient Rome and Greece. The tented theater in Miami Beach, called a "music circus," impressed her, and she told her husband, noted Broadway producer Richard Aldrich. At the time, he owned the Cape Playhouse in Dennis as well as the Falmouth Playhouse at Coonamessett.

Aldrich parlayed his previous successes to gain a buzz for his project. A piece of open field located at the intersection of Main Street and High School Road in Hyannis was chosen as the home for Aldrich's venture. Dubbed the Cape Cod Music Circus, it was the first such venue in New

The Cape Cod Melody Tent in the early 1960s. *Courtesy of Sturgis Library.*

England. The fireproof tent seating one thousand spectators held events over a ten-week summer season. Aldrich presented the high-class musicals, comedies and operas that he was used to seeing and producing on Broadway. Though they lacked scenery due to space constraints, the plays featured lavish costumes where needed and a nine-piece orchestra.

After months of anticipation, opening night of the Cape Cod Music Circus came on July 4, 1950, with a performance of Sigmund Romberg's operetta *The New Moon*. Actress Lillian Gish, comedian Fred Allen and several local politicians were among the 880 who packed the debut.

Despite the difficulty of producing weekly shows due to the lack of scenery and proximity to the audience, the first season went off without a hitch for Aldrich and his associate Julius Fleischmann. The inaugural season ended on Labor Day weekend with a performance of *Show Boat*.

In December 1950, the tent and all of its chairs were moved from Hyannis to St. Petersburg, Florida. It would be a part of the new Treasure Island Music Circus, a joint venture with music circus originator St. John Terrell. Aldrich opened another open-air music venue in nearby Cohasset in the summer of 1951, naming it the South Shore Music Circus.

Richard Aldrich, a commander in the U.S. Navy, was called to active duty in the Korean War before the start of the 1951 Music Circus season.

He was replaced in management by friend and New York lawyer David Holtzmann. The season opened with Moss Hart's *The Great Waltz*. The event was attended by nearly one thousand people on a cool July 2.

That success was followed by a new five-year lease signed in August to keep the Music Circus at its location off of Main Street. Aldrich also managed to keep ticket prices stable, roughly one to three dollars per show, depending on the day and time, despite costs constantly increasing. Attendance remained high. Early in 1953, though, worries arose that Aldrich could not retain the Music Circus site just off Main Street. Increasing costs had Aldrich wondering how to expand without losing the intimate setting.

Those worries were put on the back burner when, on June 16, 1953, a lawsuit for breach of contract was filed by the originator of the music circus concept, St. John Terrell, against Aldrich and Cape Cod Music Circus. Terrell claimed that in March 1950 he had agreed to help set up the Cape Cod Music Circus and produce or supply shows for a weekly fee and percentage of the gate. Aldrich's lawyer shot back that Terrell actually breached the agreement by not creating the Music Circus of America Corporation as he had promised.

While the proceedings were ongoing, the music circus was dealt a huge blow when the plot of land it resided on was sold to the up-and-coming

The Cape Cod Music Circus / Melody Tent in its original location in the early 1950s. *Courtesy of Sturgis Library.*

Stop & Shop supermarket chain. The venue would have to be moved in time for the 1954 season. Aldrich had five sites in mind but promised to stay in Hyannis.

In December 1953, the courts found in favor of Terrell. The decision forced the "Music Circus" name to be dropped. A contest was held to find a new name, and in January 1954, the Cape Cod Melody Tent was born. Shockingly, two people, Mildred Hobbs and Donald Traysor, submitted the same name and were given grand prizes of two season passes.

The Melody Tent would relocate to a piece of property along West Main Street just behind the former Dutchland Farms restaurant. The new locale had hardtop flooring, an upgrade from the dirt and grass of the old venue. It also ushered in the need for the West End Rotary to be built to account for the increased traffic. A larger tent with slender poles allowing less obstructed viewing and holding a capacity of 1,100 people was created. Fittingly, the first event at the new Cape Cod Melody Tent was fan favorite Jim Hawthorne starring in *The Student Prince*. This was followed by *Oklahoma!* The tent was off to the races.

The new venue was secured and successful, so Richard Aldrich sold his interests in the Melody Tent, leaving his attorney, David Holtzmann, in charge. Aldrich remained a consultant and stayed on as producer at the Cape Playhouse and Falmouth Playhouse until his contractual obligations ran out.

As the 1960s dawned, the Melody Tent slowly began shifting its attention from musicals and operas to shorter engagements with traditional musical acts. The establishment itself would see major upgrades. In 1975, the theater bowl was converted from wooden risers to concrete, and the aisle ways were redesigned to make viewing easier. The changes over the years allowed the Melody Tent to increase its capacity to 2,300 people. This helped make it more of a destination for some of the biggest stars in entertainment. Over the years, no shortage of legends has played under the tent, including Aretha Franklin; B.B. King; Bob Marley; Chicago; Crosby, Stills and Nash; Duke Ellington; George Carlin; Hall & Oates; Johnny Cash; Ray Charles; and ZZ Top.

The Melody Tent remains a fixture on Cape Cod more than sixty-five years after it first opened in a grassy field along Main Street. Though people may have ended up in nearby places such as the Paddock or Mari Jean's to finish their evenings, the Melody Tent became a huge part of Cape Cod's after-dark scene. Except for a brief flash by the Cape Cod Coliseum, it has remained the standard-bearer for entertainment on the peninsula.

Though beer and wine have been the main beverages sold at the Melody Tent, a visitor to the original Music Circus during its infancy in the early 1950s may have stopped off somewhere after to partake in a Tom Collins.

Tom Collins

¾ ounce fresh lemon juice
¾ ounce simple syrup
1 ½ ounces gin
club soda, to top

Preparation: Add the lemon juice, simple syrup and gin into a shaker with ice and shake well. Strain it into a highball or Collins glass over fresh ice. Top with club soda, garnish with a lemon wheel and cherry, and serve with a straw.

8.
CASINO BY THE SEA

286 Grand Avenue, Falmouth
1939–1999

In the twenty-first century, the area known as Falmouth Heights has become a very popular summer destination. In 1870, the beachfront neighborhood was born from what was then known as Great Hill. It was at that time that George Davis sold the property to the Falmouth Land and Wharf Company, which retained its rights before it ultimately fell into the hands of its president, G. Edward Smith. Over the first fifty years of the Heights' existence, land values increased more than 600 percent. Around the turn of the twentieth century, a Falmouth icon would be born, adding serious clout to the village of the Heights.

In 1901, the Casino at Falmouth Heights opened on Grand Avenue nearly opposite the Terrace Gables Hotel. The building, 80 feet long by 32 feet wide, with 184 feet of piazza, was run by Charles L. Hopson. The building was enlarged several times, eventually containing the Cottage Club, Falmouth Heights post office, a barbershop and a general store.

The Casino was completely destroyed by fire in April 1909, with Hopson immediately getting work started on the rebuild. The barbershop was the first to reopen just over two months later. The building was enlarged again in 1914 and became known as the Cottage Club, rather than the club simply being a part of it. In January 1915, Charles Hopson died, and his waterfront property would be owned by his wife. In 1937, a year after her death,

The crowded deck of the Casino in 1984. *Courtesy of Kathy Sullivan Porter.*

Hopson's son Harry purchased the Casino. It was here that the biggest changes would begin.

On July 19, 1939, after extensive remodeling, the Casino Bar at Falmouth Heights was added to the property with soon-to-be local legend Joe Miron coming down from Dinty Moore's in Boston to run the bar. Donned in a striped pullover, dungarees and a beret, Miron gained notoriety locally as his talent for caricatures became apparent. The bartender served up the drinks his customers desired and then followed that by sketching their likeness while they drank it. Beyond caricatures, Miron had skill with the brush when it came to landscapes and watercolors. By his third season at the Casino Bar, his works were being showcased at local art shows and galleries on the Cape. He rightfully earned the nickname "Painting Bartender."

In an attempt not to focus strictly on the alcohol output, the kitchen was revamped in 1940. The establishment was open until 1:00 a.m., and the bar could seat 150, so it was natural to try to incorporate food to go with the drink. Hopson also tried to maintain the "entertainment complex" feel by adding an E.M. Loew motion picture theater in 1941.

After trouble with erosion from hurricanes in 1938 and 1944, Hopson sold the Casino Bar to Worcester, Massachusetts resident William McCann in 1945. From there, the bar's popularity skyrocketed, along with that of Cap'n Joe. McCann focused on creating a positive work environment, including putting as first priority feeding the kitchen staff. McCann also supplied room and board to his employees if it was needed.

Joe Miron created a spot in the bar called "Amen Corner." It was named for those patrons who drank their fill and sat in the corner to philosophize.

It was here that Miron hung some of his favorite caricature sketches. The notoriety only grew when Miron was featured in the October 1943 issue of *Click* magazine. There, he was referred to as "Boston's bartender artist."

The popularity of the Casino Bar led to the need for a staff of twenty-seven per shift, including four bartenders. The "fun spot of the Heights" added horseshoes in 1946 and a new sun deck in 1947. Another name change occurred in 1949, when the establishment became known as Casino by the Sea. The seasonal spot's popularity continued to grow, with 1951 being reported as its most successful year yet.

Throughout the 1950s and into the 1960s, Miron continued to thrill guests with his skill as a mixologist and enthrall them with his artistic gifts. Summer afternoons routinely saw Cap'n Joe proudly shout down to the Casino's private beach via megaphone during cocktail hour, "Cocktail spree, Cape Cod fishballs!" Many guests heard it as "Cocktails free" and came running.

Things changed again in 1966, when William Sweeney Jr. purchased the property and gave it more of a nightclub feel, making it extremely attractive to college students and young adults during the summers of the late 1960s and 1970s. The Casino by the Sea experienced another swell of popularity during the golden age of Cape Cod nightlife.

Casino Bar. *Courtesy of Falmouth Historical Society.*

However, after spending nearly the entirety of the twentieth century entertaining folks at the Heights, the time came for last call. In 2000, the fading legend was purchased by developer Frank Messina. The Casino property was torn down in November 2003 to make way for the upscale Casino Wharf FX restaurant and condominiums, which still stand as of 2018.

For those wondering what it might have been like to sit and have a drink with legend Cap'n Joe Miron pouring, it is possible to replicate it with a popular drink from the 1940s, the Sidecar.

Sidecar

1 ½ ounces VSOP (Very Superior Old Pale) Cognac
¾ ounce Cointreau
¾ ounce fresh lemon juice

Preparation: Shake and strain ingredients into cocktail glass coated with sugar and filled with ice. Garnish with a piece of orange peel.

9.
CHATHAM SQUIRE

487 Main Street, Chatham
1968–present

Cape Cod is home to several beautiful Main Streets that run through the center of town. Hyannis, Falmouth and Chatham are among them, with Chatham's Main Street boasting an incredibly quaint village feel. Among the delightful shops and restaurants running along both sides of the street is a spot that has been drawing people in droves for five decades. It is the Chatham Squire, and it is still going strong.

The history of the business at 487 Main Street began in 1937, when a shop formerly owned by James Quilty was purchased by Arthur Drane. He opened the New York Sandwich Shop and Restaurant, counting on his reputation from his well-known Harwich Port Sandwich Shop to bring in customers. It was later owned by Charlie and Estelle Apoulas, who split time between Chatham and Miami, Florida. In 1969, a group purchased the spot and renamed it the Chatham Squire. Among the owners were Ben Lambert, who had worked at New York Restaurant, and George Payne and Richard Costello, who were only twenty-seven and twenty-six years old, respectively. The first chef was Richard's brother Michael Costello, who was the former executive chef at Executive Suite in Boston.

The new owners had the interior designs custom-made to give the allure of an old English inn. The dining area was furnished with captain's chairs and tables, mahogany-stained walls adorned with prints by artist Bill Crockett and thick carpeting in shades of green and orange. In

The Chatham Squire in 2018. *Courtesy of Christopher Setterlund.*

order to maximize their entry into the service industry, in May 1969 the new Squire not only offered high-quality food and drink inside but also offered takeout and catering, unusual for that time. The move worked, and the next year, the Chatham Squire expanded, taking over the rest of the building, which had been occupied by other businesses, including the Belfry and Margaret Valentine Sportswear. The new addition to the establishment included a cocktail lounge known as the Boathouse Lounge, with a bar that resembled a pier. Two buildings located behind the Squire were leveled to make room for more parking, completing the fledgling spot's expansion.

The success of the Squire in the food and drink realm led the ownership to begin adding entertainment to the docket. In May 1974, their attempt to receive a permit for live music was denied and would be again in March 1976. In the meantime, they increased patronage with such ideas as the Sunday Supper Buffet, which included lobster and roast beef among other delicious choices. In fact, throughout the initial years of its run, the Squire was known more for its food and atmosphere than anything. The seafood, steak and chicken dishes were mouth-watering enough to have made the establishment legendary if the ownership had so chosen to simply ride that wave. They were serving roughly 25,000 meals during its seasons by the early 1980s, after all. However, the place "where friends get together" would cement its legacy in other ways as well.

The Squire was the first spot in Chatham to have its seasonal liquor license extended from November to January, in 1978, a huge coup for business. It also increased visibility by its participation in the Chatham Harbor Run road race, with owner Richard Costello starting the race several times and the pub itself serving as the meeting spot for many runners after the festivities ended. The increase of the establishment's popularity in town paid off as, finally, in May 1982, the owners were granted an entertainment license, allowing for live music and changing the trajectory of the Squire permanently.

Above all else, it has been the atmosphere and small-town feel of the Squire that has kept people coming back. The unique feature of countless license plates and other memorabilia adorning the walls sparks conversations. Customers and staff have long-term relationships with the Squire. Many employees have worked there for decades or left and returned; some even met their spouses while working together. The sense of symmetry and reliability in the staff and the product at the establishment has resulted in many a night when the lines stretch out the door to Main Street.

As of 2018, the Chatham Squire is celebrating its fiftieth anniversary, with both Richard Costello and George Payne still at the helm. Today, the establishment is an icon of Chatham, ingrained in the culture and as synonymous with the town as Chatham Bars Inn or the Chatham Lighthouse. The Squire is open year-round and is known equally for its menu and its entertainment. One step inside the building, and it becomes apparent why this spot continues to flourish after half a century while so many other eating and drinking establishments have come and gone.

Someone paying a visit to the Chatham Squire in the decade when it finally received its entertainment license, the 1980s, may have partaken in a popular drink of the time, the piña colada. One did not have to be caught in the rain, or in the dunes on the Cape, to enjoy it.

Cape Cod Nights

Piña Colada

2 ounces dark rum
2 ounces fresh pineapple juice
½ ounce fresh orange juice
¼ ounce fresh lime juice
2 ounces coconut milk
1 ounce heavy cream
¾ ounce Demerara simple syrup

Preparation: Pour all of the ingredients into a shaker filled with ice. Shake well for a good thirty seconds and strain it into a cocktail glass. Garnish with a wedge of fresh pineapple.

10.
THE COLUMNS

401 ROUTE 28, DENNIS
1962–1984

Elegant, beautiful, mysterious and charming. These words describe the historic Greek Revival–style house situated at 401 Route 28 in West Dennis. There are three chapters in the history of this structure. For many of the younger generation on Cape Cod, this white building, with its decaying façade and unkempt landscape, is an eyesore, something that could be seen as a place where scary movies take place. It is a place to be observed from farther away with a wary eye.

For generations long since gone, it was something completely different. This was the stately home of Captain Obed L. Baker. Born in 1817, Baker went to sea at an early age and was a ship captain by the age of twenty. His legacy on the ocean is undeniable. At the age of thirty-two, Baker became a master mariner, a highly regarded term originating from the thirteenth century in England and its territories depicting someone as a master of their craft, in this case, seamanship. Baker commanded a three-masted schooner called *Luther Child*. Owned by the Philadelphia Steamship Line, it was the first American ship to visit Malta Harbor off the coast of Italy.

In 1862, Captain Baker built his home on fifteen acres of property. The home, more than five thousand square feet, was known as Elmgate. Inside, it had marble fireplace mantels, French chandeliers, an elegant carved wooden staircase banister that led to the second floor, delightfully colored carpeting, damask draperies and Brussels lace curtains. Outside,

The Columns in the late 1950s/early 1960s. *Courtesy of the Dennis Historical Society.*

it showcased a gable roof and, most striking of all, a half-round portico of columns that had been shipped from Boston in freight cars.

This home was the site of the marriage of Captain Baker's daughter Rebecca May in 1892. The captain passed away in 1895. Rebecca added glass wings to the house just after the turn of the twentieth century. She lived in the house until her death in 1957. The property was sold several years later, and the stylish yet residential home was transformed into something completely different.

The middle chapter of the home at 401 Route 28 is the most well known of the three. It began in 1961, when Stewart Wallen, formerly of Wellesley, Massachusetts, purchased the Elmgate property, which had been owned by the Baker family for nearly a century. Wallen, who had previously run the Four Seasons restaurant in New York City, christened the home "the Columns" and reopened it as a restaurant in the summer of 1962. Most of the artifacts and furnishings of the Baker family home were preserved by Wallen in a museum at the new restaurant as he tried to stay faithful to those who had preceded him. The Columns served dinner in the elegant first-floor dining area and alerted people passing by on Route 28 with a sign that read "Serving the Evening Meal."

The Columns in 2018. *Courtesy of Christopher Setterlund.*

Wallen sold the Columns in 1970 to jazz aficionado Warren Maddows. This transaction took the restaurant into a whole new stratosphere of popularity and began a shift in which the entertainment aspect of the Columns caught up to and perhaps even surpassed the restaurant aspect. With the connection Maddows and his wife, Byrle, had to jazz music, Maddows turned the Columns into a swinging jazz club. He hired Marie

Marcus to be music director of his new enterprise. Marcus was known as Cape Cod's "First Lady of Jazz" and had appeared on the original *Tonight Show* with Steve Allen in the 1950s. She had played at another legendary establishment, Mildred's Chowder House, in Hyannis in 1963 for a short time with Jim Blackmore, whom she had met doing a show at the Coonamessett Club in Falmouth.

The star power of Marcus led to many well-established jazz artists coming to play at the Columns, mostly in the Victorian cocktail lounge. Pianists Dave McKenna, Earl "Fathia" Hines and Teddy Wilson; saxophonist Scott Hamilton; and trumpeter Lou Colombo all performed on the ballroom floor at one point or another. Owner Maddows would even join McKenna on stage at times to sing, as he did have a fabulous voice. From 1970 until 1976, the Columns was the place to be for great jazz on Cape Cod. It was even home to an annual jazz festival during that time.

However, the establishment could not seat that many people, even after an outdoor tent and deck section were added by Maddows in 1977. That, coupled with patrons frowning on a small entertainment fee, meant there was not enough money being made from the jazz shows to pay for such great entertainers. It would be the beginning of the end for the Columns.

After Warren died after a long battle with lymphoma in August 1978 at the age of fifty-one, Byrle sold the Columns to jazz bassist and Boston native Ron Ormsby in 1979. Ormsby pushed the jazz club side of the Columns again, immediately promoting the return of live jazz on Tuesdays, Wednesdays and Thursdays.

Ormsby ran the establishment for a few years before it was closed in 1984 and eventually sold at auction in 1987. Despite extensive restorations undertaken in the years since the sale, the lights have remained off at the Columns. Several people and groups have come in with high hopes of opening something new inside the 150-year-old former sea captain's home. But as of 2018, the home remains stoically quiet as thousands of cars pass by it daily on Route 28.

If one had visited the Columns in its heyday as a jazz club in the 1970s, one may have partaken in a popular drink from the jazz club era called the Clover Club.

Clover Club

2 ounces gin
1 egg white
½ ounce fresh lemon juice
½ ounce raspberry syrup

Preparation: Add all of the ingredients into a shaker with ice and shake. Strain into a chilled cocktail glass. Garnish with 3 speared raspberries. Instead of raspberry syrup, you can muddle 3 or 4 fresh raspberries and ½ ounce simple syrup (1 part sugar, 1 part water).

11.
COMPASS LOUNGE

976 ROUTE 28, SOUTH YARMOUTH
1961–1998

Located dead center in the middle of Cape Cod, the Compass Lounge's history is made up of several unique chapters. It played a major part during the golden age of the Cape's nightlife. Still today, two decades after it closed its doors for good, the name "Compass Lounge" holds a special place in the hearts of those who spent many a night there. The story of one of Cape Cod's most legendary nightspots, however, began quite far removed from the loud music and dancing it would become known for.

In 1957, the land on which the Compass Lounge would eventually stand was undeveloped. Wellington W. "Duke" Holmes purchased the land from Hervey Small and petitioned the Town of Yarmouth in October 1957 for the ability to build on the 3.26-acre parcel. His plan was to create a sixty-foot-by-one-hundred-foot structure capable of holding upward of six hundred people, with the function of the building to be a public auction house. The auction house idea was approved, although, ironically, some of the naysayers said at the time that they were worried that allowing something seemingly innocent could lead to the approval of something much more disruptive and noisy. The detractors would be proven right.

By 1961, Holmes had a new idea for his auction house building. He would create a fun and unique restaurant and christen it the Compass

Lounge. The new establishment would serve the traditional Cape Cod fare, items such as steaks and seafood. Holmes would also put up a tent in the front of the Compass. This caused controversy with the town, although he said it was more of a marquee and only placed there to provide adequate seating for guests. However, the first claim to fame of the Compass Lounge, besides the tent, was its singing waitstaff.

Beginning in 1965, a special group of singing waiters and waitresses, named The Funtastics, performed at the Compass. The group of students, which included famed baritone David Evitts from the New England Conservatory of Music in Boston, performed on the Cape while also traveling around the Boston metro area and South Shore. The group was a mainstay at the Compass Lounge until 1973. Shortly thereafter, the Compass Lounge underwent its most famous change.

In 1976, Thomas Murphy purchased the establishment and transformed the run-of-the-mill restaurant into a happening nightspot. He began to bring in tremendous musical acts to entice those who might not be in the mood simply for drinks. Revolutionary Boston rockers The Cars played a gig at the Compass when they were on their way up, while former Monkees members Davy Jones and Micky Dolenz showed up in August 1977, years after their most successful period. Local bands like The Incredible Casuals made frequent appearances, while Boston-based acts like The Stompers and The Fools made the trek to the Cape to entertain the masses. Murphy was able to bring in acts like Beaver Brown and Chubby Checker as well.

The Compass Lounge rapidly became a kingpin in the booming nightlife scene of the Mid-Cape in the 1970s and 1980s. The music and dancing brought in a certain segment of the public, while cheap drinks brought others. Tuesdays and Thursdays became twenty-five-cent drink nights (eventually jumping to fifty cents in the 1990s), while Sundays, Mondays and Wednesdays were known as two-for-one nights, with drinks served in plastic glasses. The joint was always jumping inside and outside on the patio, even around back at the Sunset Club, specifically for the underage partygoers. To avoid any confusion, wristbands were given out to those old enough to drink, to make it easy on the bartenders.

The musical acts, cheap drink nights, ladies' nights and more eventually led to an enlargement of the building. Wellington Holmes's original 6,000-square-foot building capable of holding six hundred people became 9,700 square feet and was able to hold one thousand. The Compass Lounge laid claim to having the largest dance floor on Cape Cod and perhaps the

South Shore after that. The popularity of Thomas Murphy's Compass Lounge had a price, though.

By the early 1980s, the tide was shifting. There was the beginnings of a crackdown on drunk driving. With the Yarmouth-Hyannis scene including icons like Mill Hill Club, Guido Murphy's, Rascals, Velvet Hammer and more, it was a perfect location for a new initiation. The Alcoholic Beverage Control Commission started Operation Last Call, tracking the number of drunk-driving incidents traced back to specific nightspots. The Compass Lounge ended up being at the top of the list.

Although not immediate, the effects of the Operation Last Call would have consequences. In April 1989, the Compass Lounge underwent another change. This time, the establishment was taken over by Mehdi Hosseini and Alan Kasse and renamed Kasbar, complete with a Moroccan motif and $2 million sale price. The new club attempted to add a touch of urban disco to the Cape in an attempt to give the area its first "real nightclub." It did not work; in 1993, the Kasbar was no more and the Compass Lounge had been reborn.

But this latest run would see the iconic club running out of gas. The golden age was over, and things were changing on Cape Cod. By 1995, the venerable establishment had been put up for auction by Thomas Murphy. The Compass Lounge was officially shuttered in the fall of 1996. The property was razed, and a CVS pharmacy was built there in 1998.

As one of the truly legendary establishments of the golden age of Cape Cod nightlife, the Compass Lounge has earned the love that is still shared when people talk about their times there. It may be more than twenty years since the last beach ball drink, Kamikaze night or two-for-one, but the echoes of the live music off the dance floor can still be heard in the hearts and minds of the throngs of former patrons.

A visitor to the Compass Lounge at the peak of the golden age in the 1980s may have ordered a Fuzzy Navel.

Fuzzy Navel

3 ounces peach schnapps (substituting with vodka makes a Hairy Navel)
3 ounces orange juice

Preparation: Add both ingredients to a highball glass filled with ice.

12.
DEACON'S PERCH

715 ROUTE 6A, YARMOUTH PORT
1968–1985

The Cape Playhouse in Dennis has housed hundreds of high-quality performers since its opening in 1927, and it is still going strong today. Some of the greatest of all time have graced the stage there, including Ginger Rogers, Bette Davis, Henry Fonda and many more. In addition to gracing the stage at the playhouse, most performers also graced the local eating and drinking establishments, giving these places a shot of publicity. One such establishment was given a rub from one of the most beloved stars of Hollywood, Betty White.

The Deacon's Perch, situated on historic Route 6A in Yarmouth Port, was a relatively new establishment when Betty White first walked through its doors in 1968. She and her husband, Allen Ludden, were performing in the show *Bell, Book, and Candle* at the Cape Playhouse, located a little more than two miles from Deacon's Perch. The couple had discovered the bar after a show, and it became their favorite spot to unwind after performing. They would enjoy a drink and some steamed clams while listening to blind piano player Tommy Sullivan amaze them with his talents. The ringing endorsement by the Hollywood stars helped Deacon's Perch bring in the crowds, and they would keep coming thanks to another legendary piano player.

The design of Deacon's Perch was the brainchild of Leonard Healy of Boston. It would have a Victorian décor, a sharp contrast to most typical

Historic Bars, Clubs & Drinks

The former Deacon's Perch in 2018 as Royal II. *Courtesy of Christopher Setterlund.*

Cape Cod buildings. Healy wanted an "olde English" tavern feel for his creation, adding Tiffany shades on the overhanging lamps, dark wood paneled walls and a large fireplace. The cozy atmosphere allowed people to enjoy music and drinks in an intimate setting. Though it did not serve a typical menu, Deacon's Perch had finger foods and appetizers.

Only a couple of years after opening Deacon's Perch, Leonard Healy rented his establishment out to Bob Stone, owner of the Lighthouse Inn in Dennis, in 1970. Healy focused his attention on another popular nightspot he owned, the Velvet Hammer in Hyannis. Stone left the day-to-day management of Deacon's Perch to his daughter Deb Stone Haines and her husband, Sam Haines. However, the big change that was made by the new management was bringing in Ken Manzer to play piano.

Manzer, a professor of music at Westfield State, had played the Lighthouse Inn in West Dennis and Wequassett in Harwich before bringing his talents to Deacon's Perch. It was a coup for Stone, as Manzer was often referred to as a pied piper—his fans would follow him to wherever he played. Manzer played Deacon's Perch six nights a week, enthralling crowds with his talents, which were on full display thanks to the ingenious idea of putting a long mirror above the piano so everyone could see his hands while he played. Though he drew in the crowds, they often were so focused on his playing that they would forget they were at a bar and did not drink as much. Still, the idea paid off, and in 1973, Bob Stone purchased Deacon's Perch outright, with Deb and Sam Haines running day-to-day operations.

Patrons enjoyed a lot of crème-based drinks, such as Grasshoppers, Golden Cadillacs, Cremesicles and Brandy Alexanders. The crowds also enjoyed Stingers, a Cognac-based cocktail, and Dewar's, especially when Ken Manzer played. So dedicated to the experience of Manzer's playing were the folks at Deacon's Perch that the bartenders would step outside to shake drinks during his performances. In fact, Barbara Stone Amidon, Bob Stone's daughter, tells of there being at least one fistfight due to someone talking during Ken's performance. For the most part, stories of Ken's performances were more akin to the woman who would crawl under his piano so she could "feel the music washing over her."

Though not having a true kitchen, Deacon's Perch occasionally held weddings and cast parties for those at the Cape Playhouse. The food, Amidon says, was brought in from the Lighthouse Inn. The 1970s and early 1980s saw continued success for Deacon's Perch.

Barbara and her husband, Marc, opened Bishop's Terrace in Harwich on New Year's Eve 1984, signaling the beginning of the end for Deacon's Perch. That year was the establishment's last full season. It remained open only part time in 1985 so that it could retain its liquor license. During that summer, Ken Manzer began playing at Bishop's Terrace, where he continued to draw crowds through the summer of 1997. The joke was that Manzer had graduated from a deacon to a bishop.

Ken Manzer added to his legacy during his time playing at the two local hot spots by being a soloist with the Boston Symphony Orchestra and the Boston Pops, Cape Cod Symphony and Springfield Symphony. He passed away in January 2000. The Stone family sold Deacon's Perch in the fall of 1985. Today, it is home to Royal Pizza II.

Those who frequented Deacon's Perch to listen to Ken Manzer may have partaken in a Stinger Cocktail.

Stinger

2 ounces Cognac
1 ounce white crème de menthe

Preparation: Add the ingredients into a shaker with ice and shake. Strain into an old-fashioned glass over crushed ice.

13.
GUIDO MURPHY'S

615 Main Street / 16 Sea Street, Hyannis
1979–1999

The West End of Main Street in Hyannis has seen its share of legendary nightspots. From the original king, the Panama Club, in the era of World War II, to current establishments keeping the bright lights shining, this area has been continuously jumping for nearly a century. Perhaps no other spot epitomized the raucous nights on the West End like Guido Murphy's.

Long before it was a popular nightspot, the building at 615 Main Street housed the Hyannis Theatre. Originally, the three parcels of land were home to the dwelling of Albert Bacon as well as a storefront. The family sold the land, and the house was demolished to make way for a new theater. The storefront remained. The first theater opened in 1919 but did not gain traction until a second theater opened on the spot in 1923. The land on the corner of Main and Sea Streets housed not only the theater but also two stores at ground level, including the beloved St. Claire's Candy Shop in the 1920s, and apartments on the second floor. The multi-use aspect of the building would be a recurring theme throughout its history. First run by George Moore, the Hyannis Theatre built a legacy over a half century in business. But the second life of the former Bacon family property may have been equal to the first.

In the late 1970s, the entire property became known as the West End Marketplace, an indoor marketplace with several shops and food outlets. It was during this era that 615 Main Street was joined by the neighboring building at 16 Sea Street. Once this move was made, it was time for the property to take on its most famous—or infamous—form. In 1979, the former Hyannis Theatre was christened Guido Murphy's, and an icon of Hyannis's Main Street was born.

Upon its entry into the Cape Cod culture, Guido Murphy's seemed much like any other restaurant and bar. It was dark yet inviting and served a regular menu of food to entice hungry and thirsty visitors alike. What made the establishment unique during its infancy was its reliance on the fictitious Guido Murphy himself. The menu had items centered on a mix of Irish and Italian cuisine. One could sample unusual tastes, such as a corned beef and mozzarella cheese quiche, a corned beef sandwich grilled with cheese and bacon known as the Cousin Clancey from Chelsea and Don Mangatutti's turkey and mortadella, a high-quality sibling to bologna. There was also a Guido Murphy signature drink that mixed amaretto and Irish whiskey.

In 1981, the fledgling establishment was bought by brothers Frank and Tony Viola, who would take Guido's to the next level. They created Guido Murphy's Back Room with the entrance through the Sea Street property. This spot would gain an identity all its own. The lines to get into the Back Room were often so long that it became wise to arrive early and get your hand stamped, allowing access for the rest of the night. With an outdoor bar and an upstairs balcony commonly referred to as the "holding tank," the Back Room at Guido Murphy's became the place to be and to be seen. So popular was Guido's that underage partygoers scaled the neighboring building in order to drop in on the second floor of the Back Room. By 1984, Tony Viola had purchased adjacent property for parking to ease the congestion in the area, as patrons wandered out into the streets en masse upon leaving. The nickname "the snakepit" seemed appropriate for Guido Murphy's Back Room according to those who frequented it, as there was often barely enough room inside for one to raise their drink to their lips.

The popularity of Guido's eventually led to complaints by neighbors, which then caught the eye of the state's Alcohol Beverage Control Commission and its Operation Last Call. During the initial crackdown by police against drunk driving, Guido Murphy's had the second-highest number of arrests on record for the Cape, behind only the Compass Lounge. Complaints of noise, public urination and overall rowdiness after hours meant that the popular nightspot had a bull's-eye on its back from then on. Many nights, a police cruiser was parked out front in anticipation of what was to come.

There was a continuous battle between the Violas and Barnstable, as the town wished to alter the closing time from 1:00 a.m. to 11:00 p.m. to thwart as much of the late-night trouble as possible. The Violas kept up efforts to stop the problems internally; they admitted that earlier closing times would severely cut into their bottom line. Finally, in the early 1990s, the town won, and Guido Murphy's hours were cut back. As predicted, business suffered.

In 1996, the establishment underwent a bankruptcy reorganization, which led to the decision to change part of the building into a fine-dining restaurant while maintaining the Back Room. Shortly thereafter, the Italian-style spot Amici's was born. No longer seeing it as a troublesome spot, the town reinstated the later closing time of 1:00 a.m. However, an inspection in 1998 revealed that Amici's looked and felt much like Guido Murphy's. When management petitioned the town to change the name back to Guido's, the town agreed and then immediately slashed the hours back to 11:00 p.m. The financial implications caused the Violas to file for bankruptcy in 1998. There was one last ace up their sleeves. In 1999, the establishment was renamed Guido Murphy's Cabaret, complete with bikini dancers and blacked-out windows. Toeing the line very close to being a strip club, including bringing in strippers from a Florida club, Guido's finally was laid to rest by the town when its license to operate was taken away in August 1999. The infamous Guido Murphy's was dead.

The legacy of Guido's left a bad taste in the mouths of the town's residents, and for several years after. The property was sold to Jack Hynes, who remodeled the building into condos. It would be another decade after Guido's demise that another nightspot, Seaside Pub on Main, would open. As of 2018, it is still going strong. But it has a long way to go to match the lasting legacy created by Guido Murphy's and its Back Room, one of the true kings of Cape Cod nightlife.

If one visited Guido Murphy's Back Room during its heyday in the early 1980s, in addition to partaking in a Guido Murphy mixed drink of amaretto and Irish whiskey, one may have ordered a shot called the B-52.

B-52

⅓ ounce coffee liqueur
⅓ ounce Baileys Irish cream liqueur
⅓ ounce Grand Marnier liqueur

Preparation: Layer the three spirits in a shot glass in the order they are listed.

14.
HIGGINS TAVERN

151 ROUTE 6A, ORLEANS
1829–1860

Today, a bar or pub is commonly a spot to relax and unwind with friends after work. It is a place to stop in on the way home. In the nineteenth century, a bar was commonly called a tavern and was not only a spot where one could grab a drink; sometimes, it was also a place to spend the night. Typically, with these establishments, the barroom would be on the ground floor with rooms to rent on the upper floors. The oldest tavern on Cape Cod stood on Great Island in Wellfleet and is believed to have been in operation as early as 1690. In the eighteenth and nineteenth centuries, taverns that doubled as boardinghouses became more common. On the Cape, one such historic tavern stood on Route 6A in Orleans. It first opened in 1829 and belonged to Simeon Higgins.

Simeon Higgins was a ship captain in the early part of the nineteenth century. He captained the sloop *De Wolfe* in 1820 and, more importantly, captained a packet boat. The packet service involved mail being delivered by sea, which occurred until 1823, when the Admiralty, originally known as the Office of the Admiralty and Marine Affairs, took over the service until disbanding it in 1850. Higgins sold his packet boat in 1829 and set up a tavern and hotel in his home on his nineteen acres of land along the old county road, now known as Route 6A. The hotel had room for eighty weary travelers. In addition, Higgins became Orleans postmaster in 1837.

Historic Bars, Clubs & Drinks

Old Higgins Tavern, circa 1908. *Courtesy of Sam Sherman, SamsScrapbook.com.*

Stagecoaches from Yarmouth stopped at Higgins's home, dropping off and picking up sacks of mail.

The Higgins Tavern was a popular stop, catering to stagecoaches in the years before other modes of transportation existed on the Outer Cape. The first train station would not be built in Orleans until 1865, when rail service was extended from Yarmouth out to Orleans. Simeon Higgins also ran a general store out of the building and had horse stables. The Higgins Tavern was a primitive one-stop shop and gained a reputation as one of the best hotels on the Cape, in addition to one of the best taverns.

The tavern gained permanent fame when Henry David Thoreau stayed as a guest in October 1849. This stay was during his walk of the Cape's beaches, chronicled in his book *Cape Cod*, published in 1865. Thoreau's mentor and fellow author Ralph Waldo Emerson also paid the tavern a visit in subsequent years.

The time needed to run three successful ventures under one roof, in addition to turning his nineteen acres of barren land into a sustainable farm, began to take its toll on Higgins. In 1850, he sold off the mail delivery from Wellfleet to Provincetown mere months after obtaining the contracts to deliver mail from Yarmouth to Provincetown. His positive reputation kept growing, though, including holding an "open house" during one of the first Cattle Shows in 1851, held in Orleans by the Barnstable Agricultural Society, which has run the Barnstable County Fair since 1844. In July 1860, Higgins leased the hotel to John Barker as Higgins's health was failing; the tavern side of the business would be phased out. Barker closed the business the following April before it was reopened by L.D. Young in May. Simeon Higgins died only six months later, in October 1861, at the age of sixty-five.

Young would run the establishment for only six years, selling to James Chandler in December 1866 with the focus being mainly on the hotel. Chandler made improvements to the furnishings and added fishing and hunting trips as options for guests. The creation of the aforementioned railroad station in Orleans severely affected the business of the hotel and tavern. It ended up as a relatively failed venture for Chandler.

The Higgins Tavern continued operating as a hotel and again as a hardware store owned by Fred Pierce in the 1920s. However, it would see a second life as a tavern beginning in 1933. Prescott "Bud" Cummings opened the Aquanon Club in Simeon Higgins's old hotel after the repeal of Prohibition. Cummings was alleged to regale his customers with stories of rum-running with other Cape Codders in the Prohibition years.

The Aquanon Club was a success a century after the Olde Higgins Tavern had begun operation. Its time was short-lived, though. On February 12, 1942, the club and, therefore, the famed Higgins estate was virtually destroyed by fire.

Though it no longer exists in its original form, the Higgins Tavern lives on in the fact that the Olde Tavern Motel was built from part of the skeleton of the original building and stands on the old Higgins estate. It holds a deeper connection to one of the original Cape Cod taverns, which ran so successfully nearly two centuries ago.

Olde Tavern Inn & Motel stands on the site of the former Higgins Tavern. *Courtesy of Christopher Setterlund.*

Someone traveling via stagecoach who decided to stop in for a drink at the Higgins Tavern in the mid-nineteenth century had several typical libations to sample. There were spirits like brandy, whiskey and gin. However, if a mixed drink was on the menu, it would have been possible to enjoy a Sazerac Cocktail, the world's first cocktail, created in New Orleans in 1838.

Sazerac Cocktail

absinthe, to rinse
1 sugar cube
½ teaspoon cold water
3 dashes Peychaud's bitters
2 dashes Angostura bitters
1 ¼ ounces rye
1 ¼ ounces Cognac

Preparation: Rinse a chilled rocks glass with absinthe, discarding any excess, and set it aside. In a mixing glass, muddle the sugar cube, water and both bitters. Add the rye and Cognac, fill with ice and stir until well chilled. Strain into the prepared glass. Twist a slice of lemon peel over the surface to extract the oils and then discard.

15.
IMPROPER BOSTONIAN / YOUR FATHER'S MUSTACHE

626 ROUTE 28, DENNIS PORT
1967–PRESENT

A barn on the property of Joseph Baker in its former life, the Improper Bostonian has carved out more than six decades of serving suds and music to locals and visitors alike. The story of the Improper goes back to the 1960s and continues to this day as the establishment tries to provide the ultimate in nightlife to Cape Cod.

Before the Improper existed, the property at 626 Route 28 belonged to Joseph Baker. He was known throughout Dennis due to the fact that he was a trader and also ran a successful general store in the second half of the nineteenth century. Baker also owned a home in South Boston, splitting his time between the two locations. He sold his store to H.D. Loring in 1876. After his death in 1888, Baker's family remained in the stately home. Though the home itself was torn down in 1928, with pieces of it used to help construct several homes in Harwich, the barn remained. It sat empty for many years before getting a new lease on life as a nightclub.

Known as the Old Barn Club when it first was repurposed as a business in the mid-1950s, an unfortunate event several miles away would change the direction of the Baker family barn. On Long Pond in Harwich for many years sat a building that had housed several different establishments. The most well known was perhaps Storyville, the sister club to the jazz club of the same name in Boston. Storyville existed from 1957 to 1961. It was sold to Joel Schiavone, who briefly renamed it the Red Garter. Shortly

The Improper Bostonian in 2018. *Courtesy of Christopher Setterlund.*

thereafter, the club got a new name, Your Father's Mustache, and a new legacy. The name would become synonymous with a group of nightclubs connected to a collection of well-traveled and very talented musicians who to this day still tour and play their brass band music, specializing in the banjo. During its tenure, there were eleven Your Father's Mustache clubs in places like Boston, Denver, New York and New Orleans.

Your Father's Mustache, the Cape Cod chapter, began on the hill overlooking Long Pond in Harwich in 1964. It was a nightclub that once a week opened its doors to families. Sunday night was kids' night, when soda sold more than the beer. Sadly, the building burned to the ground a few years later, closing the door on the legacy the spot had built over more than thirty years. All was not lost, though.

As luck would have it, the Old Barn Club was up for sale and became a perfect spot for Your Father's Mustache to reopen its doors in the summer of 1967. The club, run by Charles "Buddy" Gould, took over the second floor of the barn; the first floor became known as the Improper Bostonian. They were separate in name yet run by the same management. It was at this new location that a Cape Cod institution was born.

In the summer of 1967, John Morgan, who had been playing down the road in Harwich at a spot called the Chuck Wagon (today, Jake Rooney's), began building his legacy of crowded happy hour gatherings here as John M. Organ. As the years went on and his reputation grew, clubs relied on Morgan to bring the crowds in. But at the beginning, Your Father's Mustache / Improper needed to rely on specialty drinks and discounts to bring the people in for happy hour.

The club kept its two names into the 1970s. It even created another alter ego with the opening of the downstairs level known as Improper Too, at Your Father's Mustache. The multilayered establishment was a seasonal, under-twenty-one club capable of packing in more than four hundred people at a time. It gained traction during the golden age of Cape Cod nightlife with things like "cheap beer night" on Mondays. But it was and still is the entertainment that brings the crowds back every season.

In addition to John Morgan, the Improper throughout its tenure regularly saw some of the Kings of Cape Cod grace its stage. Legends like Dick Doherty, who owned the Crystal Palace in Hyannis, Gordie Milne and Jim Plunkett, to more recent local stars like Grammy nominees Highly Suspect, have at one time or another plied their trade at the Improper. Plunkett as of 2018 is still rocking, doing his happy hours routinely.

In 1976, Your Father's Mustache made its way out of the old barn, and the Improper was standing alone. The Your Father's Mustache band continued to tour, but its days of running the series of nightclubs was over. The Improper became a huge part of the nightlife scene, serving up drinks and music until 1:00 a.m. all season long. As of 2018, this former barn has packed in and satisfied countless locals and visitors. More than fifty years after it first opened its doors, and more than forty years after Your Father's Mustache left the Cape, the Improper Bostonian shows no signs of letting up. It truly lives up to its claim of giving people "the ultimate in night life" and being "still crazy after all these years."

If you pay a visit to the Improper during the season, perhaps ask for a drink called the Old Rummy. The concoction is so popular that it was featured on the New England Cable News network being mixed by bar master Doug Hurley in 2014.

The Old Rummy

1 ½ ounces Cruzan dark rum
1 ½ ounces Cruzan white rum
a couple dashes of Angostura bitters
lime juice
¼ ounce simple syrup

Preparation: Mix all of the ingredients in a shaker and shake well, then pour into a highball glass over ice.

16.
JOE'S TWIN VILLA

195 Old Mill Road, Osterville
1947–2008

It had its roots during Prohibition, and its legacy was carved out from that era's folklore, splashed with an air of inclusion rarely seen during the establishment's heyday. Nestled in the quiet and affluent village of Osterville, Joe's Twin Villa became a place where everybody came together for more than six decades.

The story of Joe's Twin Villa goes back years before the three-thousand-square-foot building abutting acres of woodland became a hopping juke joint. It goes back to the days of Prohibition, when folklore has it that Joseph Gomes smuggled liquor to the building alongside Joseph Kennedy. Once Prohibition had been repealed in 1933 and liquor was again legal, Gomes had to find a new use for his building. He would find one as a coal storage area. This chapter lasted until 1947, when Gomes opened Joe's Twin Villa, beginning its run as one of the truly unique nightspots on Cape Cod.

Joseph Gomes chose the name for his establishment because his twin brother, Peter Gomes, had his own establishment, Joe Pete's, in Mashpee. It was opened as a place where the Cape Verdean and African American population of the area could safely gather and have fun. Joe's was a roadhouse with a Cape Verdean flare, with a pair of doors to get in, all dark wood inside and a beautiful mural of the Cape Cod Canal with the Bourne and Sagamore Bridges crossing it. This mural became a major influence for Joseph's grandson, Joseph Diggs, a talented and prominent Cape Cod artist.

Joe's Twin Villa began to gain notoriety for its placement in the *Negro Travelers' Green Book*. Published by Victor Hugo Green from 1936 to 1966, this guidebook featured establishments all across the United States where African American travelers could safely gather. However, despite its listing in the guidebook, Joe's quickly became a place for everyone, regardless of differences, to come together.

Joseph Gomes had the genius idea of having Thursday nights be "Maids Night." All of the women who worked in the housekeeping industry were welcomed with open arms on Thursday nights. Naturally, an influx of women meant an influx of men. Gomes invited soldiers from nearby Otis Air Force Base to come and enjoy the night. If, by chance, they were in no shape to return to the base, he would set them up in one of his cottages on Micah's Pond. The success of Maids Night spilled over to the rest of the week, and soon Joe's became the hot spot for beautiful women on Cape Cod, with the men following. The crowds gathered inside, with lines outside of people waiting to get in before the 2:00 a.m. closing time.

Gomes kept the vibe and interior of Joe's Twin Villa consistent; as Joseph Diggs says, it was a "minority idea of a social club." The only major changes during its sixty-year run came in 1978, when Joseph Diggs's cousin J.B. Richardson came to take over managing Joe's. Richardson brought in a southern style, including hardcore blues bands, the addition of items like barbecued chicken and ribs to the menu, painting the entrance doors red and adding mirrors to the walls. Boxing matches were held in the parking lot, adding to the can't-miss vibe of Joe's.

Richardson successfully ran Joe's Twin Villa for twenty-two years. It became a spot just off the radar that was all-inclusive. Everybody went to Joe's, from the everyday resident to local royalty like the Kennedy family. In fact, Joe's was such a place to be that people like John F. Kennedy Jr. would patiently wait in line to get in. Residents of all of the villages of Barnstable had corners of the bar where they'd congregate at first before comingling with the others. Hyannis Port, Osterville, Centerville, it did not matter. At Joe's, everybody was just another person.

Though they could have been treated like royalty, athletes from local sports teams such as the Boston Bruins and New England Patriots came and simply blended in with the crowd. Football legend Rosie Grier partook in festivities at Joe's, and Boston Bruins legend Adam Oates remarked to Joseph Diggs that if the Bruins won the Stanley Cup, he would bring it to Joe's so they could all drink out of it.

Old-fashioned cocktail, *Courtesy of Sam Howzit*.

Joseph Diggs achieved his dream of running Joe's Twin Villa and did so for eight years. Sadly, the long run of Joe's Twin Villa came to an end in 2008. After the Station nightclub fire in West Warwick, Rhode Island, in 2003, many new safety regulations for clubs were put into place. Diggs remarks that the cost for the upgrades were "above what the building was worth." In addition, police cracking down on drunk driving lowered the number of people going out. Finally, a change in Cape Cod's key demographic, from a younger generation in the 1970s and 1980s to seniors in the 2000s and 2010s, has meant the death knell for many local nightspots.

However, despite the end of his family's establishment, Joseph Diggs has nothing but fond memories.

"It's sad that it's closed," he says, "but the memories are all good. It was a place where everybody came together and everybody liked each other. We knew how to party and we partied hard."

If one paid a visit to the legendary "Sloppy Joe's" in the 1960s, one may have been served a simple old-fashioned.

Old Fashioned

2 ounces whiskey
½ teaspoon white sugar
3 dashes Angostura bitters
1 dash orange bitters
¼ ounce cold water
1 brown sugar cube

Preparation: Add all of the ingredients to a mixing glass. Muddle to break down the sugar and stir briefly. Fill with ice, stir again and strain into a rocks glass filled with fresh ice. Twist slices of lemon and orange peel over the drink and drop them in.

17.

JOHNNY YEE'S

228 Route 28, West Yarmouth
1967–1992

The 1960s and 1970s were right in the thick of the golden age of Cape Cod's nightlife boom. Numerous locations from one end to the other became landmarks and destinations. Some nightspots leaned heavily on live entertainment; others served high-class drinks; and some even padded their resumes with a varied menu of food items. However, only one spot could combine it all. Only one spot was Johnny Yee's.

Located along a busy stretch of Route 28 in West Yarmouth, Johnny Yee's was more an experience than just a simple restaurant. It was an attraction as much as it was a place to bring the family for dinner.

Johnny Yee's eponymous restaurant on Cape Cod was not his first successful venture in the state of Massachusetts, or even on Cape Cod for that matter. In 1963, Yee and his business partner began their first endeavor on Cape Cod. Yee took his combination of authentic Polynesian cuisine and high-quality entertainment to Main Street in Hyannis, where he helped to create the Dragon Lite Restaurant. More than fifty years later, this spot is still open and going strong at 620 Main Street. It was a great starting point for Mr. Yee, but he knew he could do more.

Two years later, in 1965, Yee, a Chinese immigrant, opened the award-winning Hu Ke Lau Polynesian restaurant in Chicopee, Massachusetts. It was in this setting that the mix of intimate dining and raucous floor shows was developed. It was and still is a huge success, run continuously by the Yee

The former Johnny Yee's in 2018. *Courtesy of Christopher Setterlund.*

family. Hu Ke Lau remains open and running strong as of 2016 and is now a legendary establishment in western Massachusetts.

In 1967, four years after starting Dragon Lite and two years after starting Hu Ke Lau, Yee decided to branch out once again. Yee's search returned him to the Cape. Due to the high volume of traffic along Route 28, Yee focused his exploration on the Mid-Cape area. He took over the location at 228 Route 28 in West Yarmouth, formerly occupied by a place called Rooster.

In September 1967, the place was rechristened Johnny Yee's. It was a hybrid spot where the Chinese and Polynesian cuisine brought people in for lunch and dinner, while the evening shows kept them coming back. Only a few months after opening, the establishment was so successful that Yee put money into extensive improvements. The entertainment and dancing, initially occurring three nights a week, quickly moved to six nights, and Yee began to promote his spot as "Cape Cod's Most Attractive Nightclub."

The entertainment side of Johnny Yee's quickly began to rival and even surpass the quality of the cuisine. Mr. Yee reflects on that time. "We had a Hawaiian show (Hawaii on Cape Cod)," he says, "jazz bands like the Count Basie Orchestra, Bobby Rich, Jimmy Dorsey, Tommy Dorsey, Woody

Herman, Glenn Miller and more. All the big bands of that moment played at my place."

In 1969, Yee opened a second Cape Cod establishment on Route 6 in Wellfleet in a building once occupied by the C-Side Restaurant.

Perhaps the crowning achievement of the entertainment wing of Johnny Yee's is the jazz album recorded there. In 1970, an album entitled *An Evening at Johnny Yee's* was put together featuring legends of jazz Lou Colombo, Dave McKenna and the Magnificent Seven. It included tracks like "In a Mello Tone," "Stormy Weather" and "Yellow Bird," purportedly Yee's favorite tune. The men on the album became regulars, performing at Johnny Yee's whether solo or in groups, such as The 16 Piece Band.

Johnny Yee's continued to draw hungry crowds as well as the hard-partying dancing crew throughout the 1970s and 1980s. It continued to bring in big-name jazz artists, including trumpeter Maynard Ferguson in 1975. In 1991, after decades of success, Yee went in search of another challenge, leaving the mainland United States to do so. He moved to Puerto Rico and opened a new venture called Peacock Paradise in San Juan. It was located inside the Caribe Hilton Hotel.

"It was a magnificent, splendid design," Yee fondly recalls. The next year, Yee sold his restaurant in West Yarmouth and moved to Puerto Rico. But he did not retire, or even slow down.

"I continued to branch out in Puerto Rico and Aruba," Yee says. "My journey in the food and beverage business has not finished. By 2006, I had a total of seventeen restaurants, including fast food in different malls in Puerto Rico."

Yee still has a home on Cape Cod and visits often. He even says that the Cape will be his place of retirement when that time eventually comes. As for his famed West Yarmouth restaurant and entertainment complex, Mr. Yee remembers it and his loyal customers warmly.

"We had a lot of good customers," he says. "We used to do catering for people; everybody loved our food, our place and our old-fashioned way." More than twenty years after closing Johnny Yee's, people still drive by the building and reminisce. It was certainly one of a kind.

If one had visited Johnny Yee's at its explosion onto the Cape Cod scene in the late 1960s, perhaps they would have ordered a classic Polynesian-style drink, the mai tai.

Mai Tai

¾ ounce fresh lime juice
¼ ounce rock candy syrup (2 parts sugar, 1 part water)
¼ ounce orgeat almond syrup
½ ounce orange curacao
2 ounces rum

Preparation: Add all of the ingredients to a shaker and fill with crushed ice. Shake vigorously until the shaker is well chilled and frosty on the outside. Pour the mixture unstrained into a double old-fashioned glass. Garnish with half of a juiced lime and a fresh mint sprig.

18.
LINCOLN LODGE

403 Lower County Road, Harwich
1953–1988

Cape Cod over the centuries has had a rich connection to the ocean. Numerous beautiful sea captains' homes dot the peninsula from one end to the other. Many of these have been deemed of historic significance, such as those on the Captain's Mile along Route 6A in Yarmouth Port. Some of these homes have enjoyed a second life as a piece of Cape Cod's historic nightlife, including the Columns in West Dennis, which began as the home of Obed Baker. Another such sea captain's home that went on to have a second life was a stone's throw from Allen Harbor in Harwich. It was originally the home of Captain Leonard Robbins and would go on to become the popular Lincoln Lodge in the mid-twentieth century.

Around 1833, the home was built for the aforementioned Captain Robbins. It was christened the Massachuseet Lodge for a planting field located in the area run by the Native American tribe of the same name. It was owned by three different people throughout the nineteenth century before being purchased around the turn of the twentieth century by a retired judge from Chicago named William Keough.

Keough made many changes to the home, mostly enlarging it into a stately summer manor. However, after nearly thirty years as owner of the home, Keough's life would change drastically. He was called into court in Chicago in the late 1930s in a dispute over properties he owned, battling against

Historic Bars, Clubs & Drinks

The Lincoln Lodge in the 1950s. *Courtesy of Rebecca Lufkin.*

members of notorious Al Capone's gang. When Keough refused to sell his properties, the rents were raised immensely. He went to court to appeal the rent increases. When his appeals were denied, it did not sit well with him. Keough shot and killed the victorious party's assessor in the courthouse. The retired judge was declared legally insane and sent away to an institution. Subsequently, Keough's children sold the property to the Borden family, whose dairy company still operates to this day.

It was the Bordens who took the stately manor and turned it into a rooming house. They also were the ones to give it the name Lincoln Lodge. The property was named for Joseph Lincoln rather than President Abraham Lincoln. Joseph Lincoln was an author born in Brewster who, during his career, specifically in the first few decades of the twentieth century, wrote about a fictionalized version of Cape Cod and had pieces published in such illustrious publications as the *Saturday Evening Post*. When the property was sold again in the 1940s to William Jenks, he kept the Lincoln Lodge name, assuming it was in honor of President Lincoln.

Jenks sold the lodge to Else Lufkin in 1953, and the former sea captain's home embarked on its most celebrated chapter. Lufkin and her son Robert Jr. began the process of turning the former rooming house into a popular eating and drinking establishment. The lodge's décor was cozy. Half of the establishment had half-circular couches with coffee tables facing a fieldstone fireplace and colonial wallpaper. The other half had the dining area and bar. One popular change was the addition of the "Village Fare," which was a changing buffet dinner on Saturday nights. In the late 1960s, Lufkin built a two-story motel on the property known as the Mary Todd Court. This meant that visitors could enjoy an evening at Lincoln Lodge and, if desired, spend the night close by.

The Lincoln Lodge promoted its menu heavily, including jumbo shrimp, clam pie, scallop stew and southern fried chicken. It also became the Cape's only fondue restaurant, adding to the popularity and uniqueness of the lodge. Woe to those who dropped food into the fondue. According to Bob Lufkin's daughter Rebecca Lufkin-Catron, there were specific instructions on how to rectify their mistake. "A waitress would bring that customer a box with slips of paper with instructions for the customer," she explains. "These would include instructing he or she to sing a song, tell a joke, recite a poem or kiss the host or hostess."

Bob Lufkin promoted an air of fun and camaraderie at his spot. This included Hawaiian luaus on the outside lawn, where a hula dance instructor was onsite to teach the dance to patrons. Rebecca Lufkin-Catron describes another way of bringing strangers together, Nut and Bolt Night, which began after 9:00 p.m.

"A guy would be given a bolt and a gal a nut as they came in the lodge," Lufkin-Catron says, "which was a way to get people to mingle, by seeing whose nut matched whose bolt."

However, Robert Lufkin shifted the focus of his establishment in the late 1970s, when he created the hugely popular drink the Nantucket Sleigh Ride.

Lufkin created a monster with this famous drink. Although Lincoln Lodge was open for cocktails nightly until 1:00 a.m., Sunday was set aside as "Sleigh Ride Night." Rebecca Lufkin-Catron says it was so popular that on those nights people would be lined up outside all the way to the end of the parking lot just to get a taste. Due to its potency, though, Lufkin set a limit of two drinks per customer. To this day, Lufkin-Catron says that she is asked just what is needed to make a Nantucket Sleigh Ride. However, that is rightfully a guarded family secret.

The Nantucket Sleigh Ride increased the establishment's popularity, as did a new entertainment license in 1984. However, both of these positives were double-edged swords. By 1985, there was an outcry by some neighbors about overcrowding and noise at Lincoln Lodge due to its increasing business. Though Lufkin went above and beyond to try to control noise and minimize intoxicated customers, he continued to battle neighbors and local police for several years. The constant battles with the town, coupled with increased police presence in the area and shortened operating hours on Sundays, proved to be too much.

Lufkin sold his beloved Lincoln Lodge in May 1988 to Scott Sogard, who drastically changed the business, which had a history of more than thirty years of being a fun place to meet people and have new experiences. Sogard renamed it Goucho's Mexican Restaurant, which it would remain for a decade before becoming Widow's Walk Condos in 1999. As of 2018, the former Lincoln Lodge is still operating as condos.

Though the Nantucket Sleigh Ride recipe is a guarded family secret, if you paid a visit to Lincoln Lodge during its height of popularity in the early 1980s, you could have partaken in another popular drink, the Slippery Nipple.

Slippery Nipple

1 ounce Bailey's
1 ounce butterscotch schnapps

Preparation: Mix both ingredients and pour in a shot glass.

19.
MILL HILL CLUB

164 ROUTE 28, WEST YARMOUTH
1949–2008

Though there have been hundreds of nightclubs, bars and other forms of nightlife on Cape Cod since as far back as the late seventeenth century, very few locations have reached the iconic heights of the Mill Hill Club. Born out of a restaurant that debuted in the mid-1920s, and standing atop Mill Hill for more than five decades, this was more than a bar, more than a nightclub. This was a destination and a landmark. It was an institution.

The history of the Mill Hill Club must be traced back to its predecessor. Nearly thirty years before the king of Cape Cod entertainment opened, another business sat atop the hill, overlooking what is today known as Route 28. In the summer of 1924, a restaurant opened its doors. It was called Old Mill Tavern, and it would carve out its own niche.

Old Mill Tavern was owned by Rose Klous, who based her restaurant on the idea of "traditional Southern cooking." This was further stressed by the fact that advertisements from the day proudly trumpeted the fact that it had a real "Southern Mammy" cooking the meals, such as chicken and waffles. The 1,600-square-foot establishment came complete with a 12-foot piazza and enticed passersby in a time when automobiles were very much still a luxury. Klous eventually sold Old Mill Tavern to Henry Fern, who ran the restaurant until his death in 1941. His death, and the outbreak of World War II, effectively ended the tenure of the establishment, which stood dormant for most of the 1940s.

Historic Bars, Clubs & Drinks

The letter board of the Mill Hill Club facing Route 28. *Courtesy of KingsofCapeCod.com.*

In the late 1940s, the most famous resident of Mill Hill took root in the former restaurant building, and Cape Cod was forever changed.

In the beginning, the Mill Hill Club was far different from how it would be viewed in its heyday. It was originally owned by Harold Smith, whose son Jack Braginton-Smith eventually owned Mill Hill, Sandy Pond Club and, later, Jacks Outback. Mill Hill was an upscale establishment hosting fancy gatherings, weddings and other parties while also having an orchestra.

Though it was known more for strings and suit jackets in the 1950s, the initial incarnation of Mill Hill Club did play a big part in the early days of Cape Cod jazz. It was during the early 1950s that legendary jazz trumpeter Lou Colombo got his start on the Cape by commuting from Brockton to play as part of a big band ensemble at Mill Hill. In the 1970s, he got a full-time gig there, leading to him moving to Cape Cod permanently with his family.

Though still maintaining a finger on the pulse of Cape Cod jazz in its early decades, the Mill Hill Club began to incorporate other forms of music inside its walls. Purchased in the late 1960s by Carmine Vara, the club ushered in acts like folksingers Peter, Paul and Mary. Later, in the days of punk in the early 1980s, Black Flag would blister through a set. Comedian and future Crystal Palace owner Dick Doherty began to perform on the Mill Hill stage. In addition to those performances, stars such as Jonathan Edwards, B.B. King, Gary Lewis and the Playboys, The Grass Roots, local legends The Incredible Casuals and more made appearances. So legendary were the live sets at the Mill Hill that, in 1979, a live album was released.

Vara, along with his son Henry and manager, Corydon Litchard, oversaw the most prosperous and yet controversial period of the Mill Hill Club. From

The disco ball from the Mill Hill Club, now located at Mill Hill Residence. *Courtesy of Christopher Setterlund.*

1969 to 1978, the same management team was in charge. That changed when Litchard left at the beginning of 1979 to try his hand at owning the venerable Velvet Hammer in Hyannis.

The Mill Hill Club was one of the pioneers of the Cape Cod happy hour and attracted thousands of people yearly, especially in its peak period of the 1970s and 1980s. The club expanded from its original 1,600-square-foot space of the old tavern to an enormous 8,500-square-feet, plus parking for 150 vehicles. It truly was the king of Cape Cod clubs.

But its popularity became a problem. Experiencing liquor violations, small fires, rowdy crowds and increasingly louder entertainment, Mill Hill became a target of the town. Beginning as early as the late 1970s, residents complained to the town about overflow parking, with people parking vehicles wherever they could just to get into the iconic establishment. Liquor and entertainment licenses were temporarily suspended at times, as in 1983 and 2001. But the club soldiered on. Henry Vara took full control of the club from his father in late 1985, with Jim Liadis coming on as manager. Henry introduced the appropriately named Mill Tavern at the Mill Hill Club as part of the complex.

At the dawn of the twenty-first century, complaint calls continued to rise, and the Mill Hill slowly slid into obscurity. Though it remained technically open until 2008, the club was virtually deserted in the years leading up to its official demise. The shell of the once mighty Mill Hill Club fell into disrepair, sitting on high, overlooking Route 28 as a relic of the golden age of Cape Cod nightlife.

The façade crumbled over a period of several years before the building was finally razed in 2014, making way for a senior living facility, Mill Hill Residence, owned by Maplewood. Opening in August 2017, this retirement community sits where the former king of Cape Cod nightclubs stood for more than five decades. In a piece of irony, the disco ball that hung inside the Mill Hill Club for decades now sits in the lobby of Mill Hill Residence, enjoying its retirement.

Those who frequented the Mill Hill Club during its peak years may have had the chance to sample an Alabama Slammer, a drink that was popular beginning in the 1980s.

Alabama Slammer

1 ounce Southern Comfort
1 ounce sloe gin
1 ounce Amaretto
2 ounces fresh orange juice

Preparation: Add all of the ingredients into a shaker with ice and shake. Strain into a highball glass over fresh ice. Garnish with an orange wheel and a cherry and serve with a straw.

20.
MILL HILL PAVILION

175 Route 28, West Yarmouth
1917–1929

Mill Pond in West Yarmouth has seen its share of history. In 1710, a gristmill was built on its shores to produce flour and cornmeal. The most well-known resident of the area surrounding the pond was the Mill Hill Club. However, sandwiched in between the colonial history and the king of nightlife, there is another, lesser known but just as important resident of the Mill Hill area. It is the Mill Hill Pavilion. It may not be the most famous spot for Cape Cod nightlife, but it was one of the originals.

The story of the Mill Hill Pavilion goes back to 1916, when construction began. Charles Blackwell and his wife had been visiting the Cape from Attleboro for years, summering in a cottage in South Yarmouth. In 1916, he had the idea of creating a building strictly for housing entertainment. The site chosen was on the busy Hyannis-Bass River Road, today known as Route 28.

Construction lasted throughout the winter and spring. At a total cost of $15,000, approximately $340,000 today, the eleven-thousand-square-foot entertainment center was christened the Mill Hill Pavilion. June 30, 1917, was the red-letter day on which the pavilion made its grand debut.

The building was decked out in red, white and blue with America deep in the throes of World War I. More than five hundred automobiles parked outside of the pavilion, with more than one thousand people coming from as far away as Provincetown and Buzzards Bay. They were greeted by the

MILL HILL PAVILION BY NIGHT, WEST YARMOUTH, MASS.

The Mill Hill Pavilion in the 1920s. *Courtesy of Sturgis Library.*

music of a six-piece orchestra inviting them inside for the inaugural dance. The night was a rousing success. The largest entertainment complex on Cape Cod was thrust into legitimacy the following week when renowned opera singer Cara Sapin appeared as part of the Boston Grand Opera Concert Company.

Despite being initially mostly known for nights of dancing, the Mill Hill Pavilion did attract talent from vaudeville and became a spot for Hyannis and Yarmouth to hold receptions after events such as Military Field Day. Once Prohibition began in 1920, the pavilion became a place of gathering without the alcohol. Dances at Mill Hill drew crowds as large as two thousand people, packing the 80-by-140-foot structure to the maximum.

Mill Hill expanded its repertoire in 1921, when basketball games became a routine part of the schedule. The game had been invented only thirty years earlier. Hundreds of people came out to watch the Mill Hill Five take on teams from all over southeastern Massachusetts. Perhaps the most legendary game inside the arena took place on December 10, 1923. It was on this night that the Mill Hill Five took on the Brockton OKO's. The game ended in a 22–14 win for Brockton. In the crowd that evening was the iconic New York Yankee Babe Ruth. Coming off an MVP season and World Series championship, the "Great Bambino" was visiting friends in Chatham when he decided to take in the game and thrill spectators at the same time.

Another highlight of the pavilion was the annual Barn Dance, which took place in September. Promoted by George Pirrie, the third annual event drew a raucous crowd of more than 1,200. It included a beauty contest won by Montreal, Quebec native Katherine Davis. Her prize? A live pig. There also was a pie-eating contest with a first prize of three dollars, a tug of war contest and separate milk-drinking contests for gentlemen and ladies.

Another piece of Cape Cod history began in the summer of 1924. Across the street from the Mill Hill Pavilion, a new restaurant opened. Owned by Rose Klous, it was called Old Mill Tavern. Specializing in chicken and waffles, this spot lasted until 1941 and was later rechristened Mill Hill Club.

In May 1926, the building was purchased by Arthur Howard, a former motion picture director connected to D.W. Griffith. The establishment was renamed Sunkist Gardens. The atmosphere inside resembled an orange grove. The three-day grand reopening attracted more than 1,500 people. The lack of a cover charge helped the new business's popularity.

Then, in an instant, Howard was gone, and Sunkist Gardens was back to being called Mill Hill Pavilion under the old management. On August 5, 1926, Howard left behind his new establishment. Legend has it that a Ku Klux Klan rally held in a field near the building on June 17, 1926, might have caused Howard's ultimate departure, but that is not definitively known.

Upon its return, Mill Hill began to hold amateur boxing matches in 1926 sponsored by the Cape Cod Athletic Association (CCAA). In addition, there were wrestling matches, including Finnish middleweight world champion Waino Ketonen. The CCAA opened its own open-air arena next door to Mill Hill in 1927 to hold events during the summer.

The run of Cape Cod's first premier entertainment complex came to a screeching halt on November 3, 1928. On this night, the building burned to the ground. Charles Blackwell told authorities that nobody had been in the building for two or three days, and he had no explanation for the fire. Insurance covered only roughly half of the $25,000 value of the building; reconstruction was not a feasible option. By May 1929, the charred debris of Mill Hill Pavilion had been removed from the site, putting a stamp on the originator of Cape Cod nightlife. A month later, Blackwell opened a lunch room at his house along Bass River. It is not known how well this endeavor went.

In 1930, the Rainbow Ballroom and Rollerdome, a dance hall and roller-skating arena, opened across from where Mill Hill Pavilion had stood. It helped carry the entertainment flag, along with the Cape Cod Athletic

Association's open-air arena, until the Mill Hill Club came on the scene two decades later.

The Mill Hill Pavilion was an important part of bringing the Roaring Twenties to Cape Cod, with music, dancing, exhibitions, boxing and basketball, in a time when such entertainment was not commonplace. It was one of the foremost forays into nightlife that the Cape offered.

Though smack dab in the middle of Prohibition, if one had visited the Mill Hill Pavilion during its heyday in the 1920s, perhaps one could have found a place off the beaten path to sneak a drink using the popular bathtub gin called a Gin Rickey.

Gin Rickey

1 ½ ounces gin
1 lime cut in half
club soda to top

Preparation: Fill a highball glass with ice and add the gin. Juice the lime halves into the glass and drop in the juiced lime shells. Fill with club soda.

21.
OLD COLONY TAP

323 Commercial Street, Provincetown
1937–present

The term *dive bar* can be one of degradation or of endearment. It can refer to any establishment, from a cozy neighborhood pub to a dirty, worn-down building in need of shuttering. For more than seventy years, Old Colony Tap, or the "O.C.," as it is lovingly known, in Provincetown, has been called the perfect dive bar with reverence from its throngs of loyal "Wharf Rats." To have survived for so long, it is safe to say that this "dive bar" has earned its distinction for being a spot where friends can gather for a drink and enjoy a bit of history and a quirky ambiance.

In a place filled with history like Provincetown (it is, after all, where the Pilgrims first landed), it may be difficult for any business to stand out from the crowd. Commercial Street is one of the most tightly packed areas on the Cape. However, Old Colony Tap has managed to carve out its own niche and is now an irreplaceable part of the Provincetown culture.

The story of this legendary dive bar began during the Great Depression. In February 1937, a new spot owned and operated by Manuel Cook opened at 321 Commercial Street. Cook was listed as an orchestra leader, and the spot was a restaurant named Colonial Tap. Whether a typo was made by the newspaper, which reported the opening, or Cook had a change of heart, by that July, the business was known as Old Colony Tap, and it remained as such.

During the early 1930s, the building next door at 323 Commercial Street belonged to Leah Crowley and was home to the Ocean Breeze Restaurant.

Old Colony Tap in 2008. *Courtesy of David W. Dunlap/Building Provincetown.*

This was a classic seafood restaurant serving fish and lobster. In March 1944, plans were made for Old Colony Tap to move into the former Ocean Breeze. It was replaced at 321 Commercial Street by another still-operating legendary establishment, the Lobster Pot. This restaurant had opened the previous year just off of Commercial Street on the Town Wharf and needed a better location. These neighboring businesses have sat side by side for more than seventy years.

In addition to Cook, there were a few other principal owners of Old Colony Tap at the beginning. One of them, Edmund Steele, became prime representative for the bar's dealings throughout the first half of the 1940s. He would sell his stake in the business to Frank Days in late 1946 and sadly take his own life shortly thereafter, on January 6, 1947, at the age of forty-two. The legacy of Old Colony Tap nearly ended in June 1949, when a major fire occurred in the building next door. Luckily, the fire was contained. Days ran the establishment until August 1955, when Herman Janard and Leonard Enos bought it. It was at this time that Old Colony Tap was transformed into the spot it is known as today.

It was Enos who had the vision to alter the interior décor of the bar. It was after his purchase of Old Colony Tap that James Wingate Parr was brought in to paint the walls, which weren't covered with driftwood. Enos also tapped fishermen to bring in nautical bric-a-brac, including life preservers from the World War II merchant ship *Lawrence Victory*. The very low-cost redecoration set an inviting ocean theme that tourists loved. The new look was a success, and it led to bigger things.

In 1962, Old Colony Tap was enlarged when it took over the building behind it, which had belonged to the Pilgrim Club. That business had moved from Commercial Street to the outskirts of town on Shank Painter Road. At first, the town was against the change, until the owners were able to convince them that a larger Old Colony Tap would be a benefit to Provincetown. They agreed, the two buildings were connected and the Back Room, later known as the Rumpus Room, was born.

It was at this time that the O.C.'s popularity was at its peak. The random nautical paraphernalia, the dark and dingy appearance, the caricatures adorning the walls lovingly sketched by the venerable "Howlin'" Jack McDonagh and the Rumpus Room all combined to turn a dive bar into a legend. It would be the go-to hangout for local writers, poets, fishermen and others. In 2011, television network HDNet featured Old Colony Tap and its signature "Everything Shot" on a show called *Drinking Made Easy*, which featured four other Cape Cod establishments.

Today, Old Colony Tap is still going strong, eighty years since Manuel Cook first opened it next door. It is a throwback to simpler times. The Enos family has been keeping the tradition going for over six decades themselves. After Leonard passed, his wife, Lucy, ran the O.C. Then, after her death in 2007, her son Leonard Jr. took over. As of 2018, he is still the owner. The Rumpus Room may no longer exist (it was torn down in the early 1980s), but not much about the O.C. has changed over the decades. That is just the way the Wharf Rats like it.

Someone enjoying an evening overlooking the water at the newly opened Rumpus Room in the 1960s may have requested a Ramos Gin Fizz. This drink was immortalized by Tennessee Williams in many of his writings. Williams spent four summers in Provincetown in the 1940s and had a string of hits through the 1940s and 1950s, including *The Glass Menagerie*, *A Streetcar Named Desire* and *Cat on a Hot Tin Roof*.

Cape Cod Nights

Ramos Gin Fizz

2 ounces gin
½ ounce heavy cream
½ ounce fresh lemon juice
½ ounce fresh lime juice
¾ ounce simple syrup
3 dashes orange flower water
1 fresh egg white
club soda, to top

Preparation: Add all of the ingredients except the club soda into a shaker and dry-shake vigorously (without ice). Fill the shaker with ice and shake it again. Strain the mixture into a collins glass. Pour a little bit of club soda back and forth between the empty halves of the shaker to pick up any residual egg white, then pour into the glass.

22.
ON THE ROCKS

ROUTE 28, MASHPEE
1965–1982

Today, the town of Mashpee is a hub of action, due in large part to the massive Mashpee Commons shopping center which lies just off of the Mashpee Rotary. Decades ago, long before the Commons existed, Mashpee was a hub of action for a different reason. Its laws for serving alcohol differed from most other Cape Cod towns. The 2:00 a.m. closing time meant that countless partygoers from the neighboring towns flocked to Mashpee once their respective nightspots closed in order to squeeze every bit of fun out of the night. The epicenter of this flood of people was ironically just across the street from where, one day, Mashpee Commons would stand. It was On the Rocks, and for two decades it made Mashpee one of the most popular party towns on Cape Cod.

The story of On the Rocks began in the 1950s with the arrival to Mashpee of Richard and Heleana Wasil. The couple first settled nearby on Route 151, leasing Henry LaBute's Lakeside Restaurant along with a gas station and general store in 1958. The Wasils made creating businesses their business over several decades. This would include later on creating Dick and Ellie's Flea Market in South Dennis. However, their next venture came nearby when, after their success at their first restaurant, they decided to open a new restaurant on Route 28 called Helena's Backyard Restaurant. Though this was also a success, the Wasils wanted a little more. This came with a name change to Ellie's

Drift-Inn and a license to house entertainment on Sundays. The result was famed jazz singer Marie Marcus and her band making Ellie's their main summer haunt from 1963 to 1965, drawing many new faces who would become regulars. The Wasils sold their establishment in 1965, moving just south to create Dick and Ellie's Drive-In. The building was then sold to Laurence Casale, fresh out of college, who renamed it On the Rocks. The new nightspot became an instant hit.

The initial boost of popularity for the new establishment came from the wealth of musical talent that came through the doors, courtesy of second owner Chet Wright, who would also later own the Quarterdeck Restaurant in Falmouth. The talent included a young Bette Midler, along with Barry Manilow in the summer of 1971 and an appearance by James Taylor in August 1972 as he campaigned for Congressman Gerry Studds. On the Rocks gained a new swell of customers with the change of a law a few years later. In June 1974, the owners of three Mashpee clubs—On the Rocks, the Farm and Poets Pub—successfully lobbied the town for a later closing time of 2:00 a.m., later than any other Cape town would allow. This meant that those enjoying a night out in Yarmouth, Hyannis or Falmouth could keep the fun going by driving into Mashpee for last call. On the Rocks benefited greatly from this popular practice.

The new closing time, along with the drinking age of eighteen, created a wave of party seekers at On the Rocks. Wright instituted a special of five beers for one dollar on Sundays to capture new and returning patrons. On the Rocks also created a special club called the South Mashpee Sipping Society, complete with a numbered card for those locals who frequented the establishment.

Throughout the 1970s, the musical acts would continue to amaze, with legends like Kool and the Gang, Sha Na Na, Joe Cocker, J. Geils Band and Ike and Tina Turner stepping to the stage. So crowded did the musical events become that a large white tent was installed in the back with a dirt floor to accommodate all of the people. Wright sold his club in the late 1970s to Paul Kelly and Kevin O'Connell, who continued its success for a few more years.

On the Rocks was sold in 1982 to John Burke, who renamed it the Channel after a preexisting club of the same name that had opened in Boston three years earlier. The Channel would also be known as Club 55 and have a short-lived tenure. By the fall of 1984, the establishment had filed for bankruptcy and was closed shortly thereafter. The last act of the building that once housed On the Rocks was to occur in the spring of 1985. The Mashpee Fire Department used the former nightspot as a controlled burn for a training exercise on May 11, 1985. In the more than three decades since then, nothing else has been built on the property.

Today, the sprawling Mashpee Commons attracts countless customers year-round. Those who enter from Route 28 pass by a large empty lot filled with piles of sand. For many it is simply an eyesore; however, for many who lived through the golden age of Cape Cod nightlife, it is a sad reminder of the good old days when the piles of sand were replaced with a jumping entertainment and drinking establishment the likes of which will likely never be seen again, called On the Rocks.

If one visited On the Rocks during its heyday in the 1970s, he or she may have ordered a popular cocktail known as a Yellow Bird.

Yellow Bird

1 ¼ ounces white rum
½ ounce Galliano L'Autentico
½ ounce Bols Triple Sec
½ ounce fresh lime juice

Preparation: Add all of the ingredients to a shaker and fill with ice. Shake, and strain into a martini glass. Garnish with a lime wheel or a slice of lime peel.

23.
PANAMA CLUB

6 Sea Street, Hyannis
1941–late 1950s

As nightspots on Cape Cod go, there are few to rival the history or the legendary status that the Panama Club earned in its time. In the days before the Melody Tent, or even before the West End Rotary existed, the Panama Club was drawing in patrons in huge numbers to an area that at the time was not yet an epicenter for after-dark fun. It put Hyannis and jazz music on the map on Cape Cod and southeastern New England.

The story of the Panama Club began shortly before World War II landed on America's front step. It was a time shortly after the worst of the Great Depression had subsided. In those days, there were very few places for young people to get together and have a good time. That would change with the arrival of Antonio Caggiano from Boston in 1937. In 1941, he, along with his son Reynold, opened the Panama Club near the end of Main Street. Decorated in red and white velvet, this establishment ushered in a new era of nightlife on Cape Cod. It was the first swinging jazz club.

Though the father-and-son owners also operated other businesses—Rennie's Lounge in Hyannis and Rico's Restaurant in Centerville—the club on Main Street would forever etch their names in Cape history. Their Panama Club was a hotbed for the youth of Cape Cod, guys and girls dressed to the nines looking to meet up. Couples and those who had never laid eyes on each other alike would pack together on the small dance floor and get their feet moving to lively swing music.

Historic Bars, Clubs & Drinks

Looking down Main Street Hyannis with the Panama Club on the right, circa 1940s. *Courtesy of Sturgis Library.*

Not very long after bursting onto the scene, the Panama Club became an escape for locals after news hit of the attack on Pearl Harbor on December 7, 1941. Those who were in the club learned of the news while they were inside; some rushed home while others stayed. The establishment did not close, though, and it was packed again the next day, with some even bringing their own beer with them. The events of Pearl Harbor and the Panama Club would become the subject of a popular fictionalized play written by Larry Marsland of Chatham in 2006.

The Panama Club became the jumping-off point for Cape Cod's "First Lady of Jazz," Marie Marcus, who first graced its stage in 1943, when she was still billed under her maiden name of Marie Doherty. She teamed up with Alma Gates White to form the "Piano Maniacs," playing the Panama Club as well as the Coonamessett Club in Falmouth. While performing at the Panama Club, Marie met her future husband, trumpeter Bill Marcus.

The bar at the club was always packed, with beer being the drink of choice, selling for seventy-five cents. Shots of whiskey cost sixty cents. For those who did not wish to travel to the busy club, there was another way to listen to the live music being performed there. This was thanks to the occasional live radio broadcasts transmitted from the Panama Club. However, so crowded did the club become that during one show in 1943, legendary WOCB DJ Vern Coleman, then only seventeen, had to set up his equipment and broadcast the night's live music from underneath a table. The radio broadcasts remained a fixture throughout the 1940s.

As the decade passed, the club became the place to be. World War II did not dampen business. Everyone from celebrities to soldiers at Camp Edwards to the everyday worker made their way to the end of Main Street. Those who worked in the businesses nearby would get off of their shift and walk down to enjoy a drink and a chat. Many locals became well known due to their playing at the Panama Club, including pianists Mike Markaverich and Marion Cahoon, who would teach piano at the Cape Cod Conservatory of Music for three decades. The joint would be jumping until midnight, after which people poured out of the Panama Club's several exits. Some wandered down the Byway alley winding behind the club, while others simply congregated in the streets. The crowds were so large that during its heyday it was said to look like a mini Times Square outside.

The Panama Club gained perhaps its most famous regular in the form of summer resident and future president of the United States John F. Kennedy. The course of history was changed inside the walls of the club in September 1944. It was shortly after the Great Atlantic Hurricane hit the Cape that Kennedy and two female friends paid a visit to the Panama Club. They enjoyed it. It also was one of the first places to reopen after the storm. During a break between dancing, Kennedy first mentioned his desire to become a politician, specifically a potential run for governor despite only being twenty-seven years old at the time.

In the 1950s, the Panama Club saw some changes. In June 1953, the Caggianos sold the establishment to former Uxbridge Inn owner John Cornelia. There was also competition in the form of the Catalina Club, which opened at 654 Main Street. The club continued its run for a few more years before closing in the late 1950s. The building was torn down in 1972; as of 2018, the site of the former Panama Club is occupied by a Dunkin' Donuts. Only memories and scant images remain now of Cape Cod's original swinging jazz club. Luckily, Larry Marsland's play brought some light back to this lost icon.

A visitor to the Cape's original swinging jazz club in its heyday of the 1940s may have ordered a popular drink during wartime, a daiquiri.

Daiquiri

1 ½ ounces light rum
¾ ounce lime juice
¼ ounce simple syrup

Preparation: Add all of the ingredients into a shaker with ice and shake until well chilled. Strain into a chilled coupe. Garnish with a lime twist.

24.
PILGRIM CLUB / PIGGY'S

323½ Commercial Street/67 Shank Painter Road, Provincetown
1945–1981

In a town filled with history such as Provincetown, it can be difficult for an establishment to make a name for itself. It is downright unheard of for an establishment to make a name for itself, move to another part of town, change its name and find success a second time. Yet this is exactly what happened, as, in the 1940s, the Pilgrim Club opened on Commercial Street, then two decades later move to the outskirts of town on Shank Painter Road. Shortly after that, it began to be known as Piggy's. It was a nickname at first, then it became official in the early 1970s. This set off a second life for the business. How did it happen?

In the 1930s, the building at 323½ Commercial Street was home to the White Whale and Mooring Mast nightclub owned by Frances Bell. In 1939, the White Whale moved out, and the Cape End Club, owned by Milt Tremblay, moved in. The club would only last until 1943 before closing down. It remained shuttered for two years before a new club opened in the large building accessible through a narrow alleyway.

On May 26, 1945, Frank DeMello opened his new Pilgrim Club to much fanfare. It included light appetizers, drinks and an orchestra. DeMello had initially attempted to secure the property at 391 Commercial Street for a nightclub but was denied; the former Cape End Club was his backup plan. Though the inaugural season was a success, DeMello was cautiously optimistic and kept his side job of watch and jewelry repair. He doubled down on his investment and renovated Pilgrim Club in time for its second season so it could serve food in addition to its drinks and dancing. The entertainment was quite the staple of the fledgling club, with acts such as Sam Robinson's Harlem Boys, the Duke Boyce Trio and the King Levister Quartet. There was also four seasons of dance group Schatzi and Tobi performing and, later, jazz nights with several highly acclaimed acts.

In 1955, to add more variety to the club, DeMello built the Driftwood Lounge, later called the Neptune Roost. Despite having success at its initial location, the lease on the property was allowed to expire in 1962. The property was quickly scooped up by neighboring Old Colony Tap and turned into the famed Rumpus Room. DeMello had his eyes on a spot on the outskirts of town for the second act of the Pilgrim Club. In order to get the clearance to move his business over to Shank Painter Road, DeMello made concessions that the establishment would become more of a family-friendly restaurant rather than a nightclub. In March 1962, the move was approved and the Pilgrim Club took over the building at 67 Shank Painter Road, owned by Matt Costa and once known as the Hole in One.

Initially, the move less than a mile to Shank Painter Road and the conversion to a family-style restaurant stuck. Pilgrim Club promoted its Portuguese delicacies to try to increase patronage. However, it was not too long before DeMello began tweaking his agreement, as the business was slower than expected. First came an attempted addition of a jukebox to play Portuguese folk music in June 1962. A year later, in July 1963, he was granted permission from town selectmen to stay open until 3:00 a.m., though he had to stop serving alcohol at 1:00 a.m. This did not help to the degree he had hoped. Faced with a losing situation, he was soon pining for a spot on the hotbed of Commercial Street again.

DeMello petitioned the selectmen in January 1965 to transfer the liquor license of Pilgrim Club to a spot at 303 Commercial Street formerly known as the Wreck Club. After much consideration, the application was denied on the grounds that there were already eleven bars in the area surrounding DeMello's potential site. This would cause DeMello to sell Pilgrim Club to A. Philip Tarvers. The new owner would try the transfer again in 1966, with an accompanying petition signed by loyal patrons. It again was denied. Tarvers changed the establishment by making it "Members Only" shortly after purchasing it. The hopes of moving Pilgrim Club back into midtown dashed, Tarvers quickly sold Pilgrim Club in March 1967 to Thomas Rutherford.

Rutherford's first act as owner was to, for the third time overall, attempt to move Pilgrim Club. His choice was a spot at 135 Bradford Street. It was again denied. It was at the end of the 1960s that Pilgrim Club's fortunes changed, along with its name.

In the late 1960s, the Pilgrim Club was taken over by Reggie Cabral. It was under his watch that the establishment began to be called by a new nickname: Piggy's. Cabral was the latest in a rapid-fire line of mangers, though. In 1971, E.J. Smith took over, and the Pilgrim Club name vanished. The establishment on Shank Painter Road was officially known as Piggy's. Despite it technically sticking to its designation as a restaurant, thus having no live entertainment, the newly crowned Piggy's quickly became the place to be for locals.

For a few years, Piggy's was riding high as one of the hottest spots on the Cape. People from every background comingled in the dark, dingy club. The all-inclusive club brought in annual profits of close to $200,000 at its height. However, the heyday of Piggy's was relatively short-lived. The downward slide began when E.J. Smith lost a court battle to a partial investor and Piggy's bartender Louise Perry Meeks. Meeks and her husband, as well as Piggy's doorman, John Vance, took over the club from Smith and ran it for two years until 1977.

The slide of Piggy's popularity had several causes. The constant tinkering of the interior of the club, including the sound system, led to some bad vibes. There was also the incident in 1976 when the establishment had its liquor license temporarily suspended due to allegations of watering down and tampering with drinks. Third was the increase of violence in and around the club's premises, which turned off some regulars and kept away potential new customers. Finally was the increase in competition from midtown establishments like Crown & Anchor's Back Room. Whatever the major cause, the end came in 1981, when Piggy's license was revoked after a failed attempt at live music and dancing to records.

Building owner Matt Costa stepped in and leased the club to new owners, who changed the name to Dallas; then to another new owner, who changed it to La Disc. By the end of 1981, Costa had taken it upon himself to run the club, changing its name to Captain John's, named after his father. It regained a stable following in the late 1980s and early 1990s, when the club was known as the Love Shack. In 1995, Costa finally sold the property to Cynthia Gast, ending his association with the building on Shank Painter Road after more than thirty years.

From its roots as the Pilgrim Club along the water on Commercial Street to its second boom as Piggy's on Shank Painter Road, this establishment had a legendary story with two legendary chapters. As it says on David Dunlap's Building Provincetown website, Piggy's may be the last time Provincetown danced together as one.

If you stopped into Piggy's during its heyday in the 1970s for a drink, you may have asked for a drink with roots in Provincetown, and with bartender John Caine, the Cosmopolitan.

Cosmopolitan

1 ½ ounces citrus vodka
1 ounce Cointreau
½ ounce lime juice
1 dash cranberry juice

Preparation: Add all the ingredients into a shaker with ice and shake. Strain into a chilled cocktail glass. Garnish with a lime wedge.

25.
PUFFERBELLIES

183 IYANNOUGH ROAD, HYANNIS
1981–2016

One of the last true nightclubs that remained from Cape Cod's golden age of the 1970s and 1980s was Pufferbellies. Its story began in the waning years of the nineteenth century as part of the height of the nation's railroad era. The twelve-thousand-square-foot brick building that, a century later, housed a legendary and sometimes infamous club started its life in 1895 as a railroad roundhouse owned by the Penn Central company. The double-thick brick walls, which were installed to soften the sounds of the old railroad engines entering the roundhouse, came in handy when the argument for turning the building into a nightclub came into play.

Penn Central filed for bankruptcy in 1970, with much of its properties on Cape Cod going into limbo. Much of the rail line east of Dennis eventually became the route for the Cape Cod Rail Trail. The twelve acres of land located between Iyannough Road and Center Street were seen as a prime location for a revitalization of downtown Hyannis. In the summer of 1978, Leonard Healy, owner of the nearby Velvet Hammer nightclub, had attempted to purchase the land and had his offer rejected. The property went back on the auction block.

It was around this same time that a burgeoning Cape Cod legend was looking for a spot of his own. John Morgan had been supplying locals with countless hours of fun with his John Morgan Happy Hours for over a decade by the time of Healy's failed bid for the former Penn Central property.

Historic Bars, Clubs & Drinks

The façade of Pufferbellies. *Courtesy of KingsofCapeCod.com.*

Morgan had debuted on the Cape at the Chuck Wagon in Harwich in 1965 when just out of college. He moved on to the Improper Bostonian / Your Father's Mustache in Dennis Port before leasing the Sandy Pond Club in 1971 for three years and calling it the Groggery at Sandy Pond. Morgan played to crowds dotted all across New England, and these people became devotees. On Cape Cod after leaving the Sandy Pond Club, he settled in as a regular performer at Dick Doherty's Crystal Palace in Hyannis and remained for seven years. Eventually, Morgan had visions of his own nightclub and even offered to buy the Crystal Palace, but Doherty was not ready to sell. So Morgan was on the lookout, which brought him to the former Penn Central property in downtown Hyannis.

In late 1980, Morgan purchased the former railroad roundhouse from the Eldredge and Bourne Moving Company for $100,000 ($324,000 in 2018). In early 1981, he made a pitch for a new nightclub, a place where the younger generation, locals and visitors alike, could congregate. His plan was a seven-hundred-seat restaurant and club to be named Pufferbellies, another name for a steam locomotive. The new nightclub was approved. From its opening on May 8, 1981, it was an immediate hit.

"We knew it would be a home run," Morgan says, "but it turned out to be a grand slam."

The letter board of Pufferbellies along Route 28. *Courtesy of KingsofCapeCod.com.*

The 12,500-square-foot brick roundhouse had the capacity to hold 1,500 people, with a stage, three bars and even an outdoor volleyball area. Although it was seen as mainly a nightclub and bar, Morgan did receive an outside dining permit in 1983 so that, if anybody did choose to eat, they had the option of enjoying fresh air. Of course, Morgan continued to draw in the crowds to his happy hours, so popular were they that special drinks and two-for-one specials were not necessary to bring in the masses. They came to see John Morgan, sing along with him and be part of the crowd. Musical acts from Boston-based The Freeze to nationally known "Weird Al" Yankovic came down to the Cape to take the stage at Pufferbellies early on. In later years, bands like Blue Oyster Cult, Sevendust and Powerman 5000 graced the stage. The new nightclub was a hit.

One big reason for the routinely packed Pufferbellies was the advertising campaign. It was the brainchild of Morgan and local radio DJ Gary Titus. Morgan bought "a thousand ads" for play on popular Cape Cod radio stations 106 WCOD and Cape 104.7 WKPE. Titus put them together, and they hit the airways. Morgan and Titus made sure that people would hear an ad for Pufferbellies twice an hour. The campaign worked. Morgan had a staff of one hundred employees at his club dressed in button-down Oxford shirts with his nightclub's name embroidered on it. This was a stark contrast to some night spots at the time, which dressed their employees in T-shirts. Morgan's care and attention to detail paid off.

After five seasons of running Pufferbellies, Morgan was getting burned out.

"It took a lot of work to have 1,500 people come in for the afternoon," Morgan says, "and then have to get them out, clean up, and bring in another 1,500 for the night."

All of this added up to Morgan selling his nightclub in 1986 to Peter and Jeanne White, who owned the Boston Fish House, for $3.1 million. He still performed his happy hours, but as far as he was concerned, his nightclub-owning days were over. Within a few years, though, Morgan had bought back his nightclub. But the place was not the same. Without Morgan at the helm, Pufferbellies had suffered. More than that, the times were changing in the late 1980s and early 1990s.

The liquor liability laws affected business, and harsher drunk-driving penalties made patrons think twice about heading out to clubs. These were a couple of the things that led to Morgan shortening the club's schedule. For the majority of the 1990s, Pufferbellies was open just two days a week. In 2001, Morgan said that business was only "a twentieth of what it was in the 1980s." He had wanted to use the brick roundhouse building for other purposes, such as conventions, weddings or other functions, but it never came to be. The changes eating away at the club continued. In 2015, Morgan happily sold the property once and for all to the HyLine ferry for $1.96 million

At its peak, Pufferbellies was the place to go for fun and entertainment on Cape Cod. It was the last of the giants of the golden age to fade away. But John Morgan doesn't miss it. He still keeps himself busy performing his happy hours and drawing in big crowds, even now, in his mid-seventies. Morgan remains one of the kings of Cape Cod. As for what made the golden age so special? It came down to timing and circumstance.

Morgan remembers how, in the days before cell phones, everybody had to make plans to meet out somewhere. There were fewer options, the drinking age was eighteen and the large baby boom generation was in its prime. Now there is an overload of options, the drinking laws are different (the age is now twenty-one) and the baby boomers are becoming senior citizens. Times have changed, but Morgan fondly remarks, "We had a lot of fun."

If one visited Pufferbellies for a John Morgan Happy Hour in the heyday of the mid-1980s, one may have ordered an Amaretto Sour.

Amaretto Sour

1 ½ ounces Amaretto liqueur
¾ ounce cask-proof bourbon
1 ounce fresh lemon juice
1 teaspoon rich simple syrup
½ ounce egg white, beaten

Preparation: Add all of the ingredients to a shaker and dry-shake to combine. Add fresh ice to the shaker and shake again until chilled. Strain over fresh ice into an old-fashioned glass. Garnish with lemon peel and brandied cherries, if desired.

26.

RAINBOW BALLROOM

174 Route 28, West Yarmouth
1930–mid-1960s

Today, when one thinks of nightlife, it inevitably comes down to one of two things, a nightclub or a bar. But in years past, many more venues were considered part of the nightlife scene. This was most certainly the case with the Rainbow Ballroom. This unique hot spot was not big on alcohol, but it routinely drew many hundreds of locals and visitors inside its walls to partake in good fun after dinner and after sunset.

The story of this legendary establishment goes back to the Roaring Twenties, when Ernie Baker, with his Novelty Orchestra, was making a name for himself all across southeastern Massachusetts. Baker, a well-known local in Yarmouth, would often set up gigs for his orchestra at the Mill Hill Pavilion, a popular live entertainment spot located in West Yarmouth. As the 1920s went on, Baker had a plan to create a more permanent home for his musical group.

In June 1930, Baker purchased six lots of land located opposite the Mill Hill Tavern. It was on this land that he planned to build his very own dance hall to house his Novelty Orchestra. The work on the building was swift, and it was ready for its debut within weeks. The dance floor was remarked as the largest east of New Bedford. The interior was decked out in pastel colors, with white being the main shade, including a white stage and a pristine and unique white piano adorned with painted flowers.

The Rainbow Ballroom in the 1930s. *Courtesy of Sturgis Library.*

A contest was held, with more than one thousand entries, to name the new dance hall. The winning name was the Rainbow Ballroom. The winning entrant received twenty dollars and two season passes to the establishment.

Opening night for the Rainbow Ballroom was Wednesday, August 13, 1930. The crowd was so large that the enormous dance floor was packed all night. It was a state-of-the-art hot spot, with the newest in electric lighting, allowing for the lights hitting the dance floor to be changed to a variety of colors. The women's dressing rooms even including electric curling irons. Two orchestras kept the music playing all night. The debut of Ernie Baker's Rainbow Room was a rousing success.

From the start, Baker maintained a high profile for himself as well as his club. There were themed dances such as a Thanksgiving Puritan Ball and a Miss Cape Cod contest held on New Year's Eve 1930. Miss Gilbery Kelley of Hyannis Port was crowned the winner out of 250 entrants. She received a silver cup. Baker also continued to play gigs across the Cape and southeastern Massachusetts with his orchestra, undoubtedly enticing more to come and visit the Rainbow.

Baker upped his game in 1931 by adding amateur basketball in the form of the Hyannis Wanderers. Teams from all over the state came to play them. Typically, the games were held on Wednesdays during the season, with dancing happening both before and after. Ahead of his time in marketing, Baker gave away a Sport Model Chevy automobile, which he had been using for advertising the Rainbow in January 1932. His nightspot was gaining and maintaining its popularity through many different avenues. The following year, even more would be added.

The Rainbow Ballroom began throwing midnight dances, typically running from midnight to 3:00 a.m. They were occasional occurrences, which established them as must-attend events. Later, in 1933, Baker experimented with a new activity, roller skating. This became such a hit that it took place three times a week, drawing many new faces. Baker even rented out use of his building to others for charitable events and the like.

Word of mouth and positive experiences began to spread. In 1936, Chick Webb and his NBC Orchestra made an appearance at the Rainbow, fronted by the one and only Ella Fitzgerald. It was during this year that boxing debuted to add to the already popular Hyannis All-Stars wrestling bouts that took place there. In 1938, Baker and his Rainbow Ballroom saw their greatest exposure, as they were routinely promoted on the national *Old-Fashioned Cafe* radio program. Show host Ken Singer had been playing at the neighboring Old Mill Tavern and began to frequent Ernie Baker's popular establishment.

Despite hosting roller skating, basketball, boxing and wrestling, the Rainbow would remain true to its first event, dancing. Throughout the 1940s and 1950s, there were themed dances, midnight dances, holiday party dances, charitable balls and more. Ernie Baker knew what his customers wanted and gave it to them. Long after the Old Mill Tavern had gone out of business, replaced by the Mill Hill Club, Ernie Baker's Rainbow Room was still going strong.

By the mid-1960s, after about thirty-five years of ownership, Ernie Baker closed his Rainbow Room and took a well-deserved retirement. The building itself remained dormant for several years before being sold in 1970. In the more than four decades since, the familiar shell of the building has remained, housing such businesses as Quoddy Moccasins Shoe Factory Outlet, French Shriner Shoes, Clancy's Restaurant, Reebok Outlet and most recently a Salvation Army store.

But no matter what business resides on the property, it will always be fondly remember by longtime Cape Codders as Ernie Baker's Rainbow

Room. It was a unique nightspot that relied on dancing, roller skating, basketball, boxing and wrestling—everything but the alcohol—to claim its spot as a forefather of the golden age of Cape Cod nightlife.

Despite not being known for cocktails, if one had frequented the Rainbow Ballroom in its heyday for some dancing, perhaps one would have made a drink afterward at home such as the popular French 75.

French 75

3 ounces champagne
1 ounce gin
½ ounce fresh lemon juice
½ ounce simple syrup

Preparation: Add all of the ingredients except the champagne into a shaker with ice and shake well. Strain into a champagne flute. Top with the champagne and garnish with a lemon twist.

27.
RICK'S OUTER BAR

4550 Route 6, Eastham
1981–2011

The Outer Cape is home to some of the most beautiful beaches, specifically, those facing the Atlantic Ocean, such as Nauset Beach and Coast Guard Beach. These are also where one can find the biggest waves being ridden by surfers both local and visiting.

It was at Nauset Beach in Orleans where surfing legend Rick Weeks learned the craft in the mid-1960s. Though he surfed all around the world, Weeks has been synonymous with surfing on Cape Cod for nearly half a century, moving to Eastham after college to live the surf life. It was only natural that Weeks's love of surfing was parlayed into a business centered on the craft. It was called Rick's Outer Bar and was a shrine to the surf culture and the legendary character Rick Weeks.

Rick's Outer Bar was created from the ground up by Weeks himself as he took a small twenty-by-forty-foot space that had been used as living quarters by the previous tenant and completely revamped it with his own two hands. He literally built the tables for the bar out of reclaimed yellow pine and bought the chairs and a used three-door reach-in refrigerator. He brought in his own stereo but initially desired to keep the bar television-free to enhance the conversation. The walls included many photos showcasing Weeks's surfing exploits throughout the world. In all, it took barely a month to go from zero to operational, and Rick's Outer Bar debuted on May 8, 1981.

The bar was just what was needed in Eastham. It was a place for the locals to go, which was what Weeks wanted.

"It was always intended to be a local bar," Weeks says, "because that's what I was and that's what I knew." With no sign on the busy Route 6 and no advertising being done at first, the establishment relied on repeat business from loyal locals to make the first year a success. In the beginning, it would consider itself a "warm up bar for the Beachcomber," but that would soon change.

Besides the surf décor and the small, intimate setting, what set Rick's apart was the music. Weeks painstakingly made mixtapes during the days of cassettes and later on made mix CDs of music from all genres. He also undertook a $5,000 spending spree in one fell swoop. It was known as "Rick's Music," described by Weeks as "content mixing." In the early days, people danced by pushing aside tables and making the best use of the small space. Later on, the bar gained a twelve-by-twenty-foot addition for a dance floor and DJ booth. The inclusion of alternative music in the 1980s may have dismayed some of the old-school characters who enjoyed Rick's Outer Bar, but it introduced people to music they may have not otherwise heard, bringing the close-knit regulars even closer. The radical idea of Rick's Music had club owners from Boston willing to pay Weeks to come and teach their DJs to replicate his playlists.

Eventually, Rick Weeks relented and began radio advertising, writing and performing hundreds of his own ads over the decades. The result was booming business, which made the bar's size come into play. When the business next door became available in 1989, Weeks pounced and bought it. He carefully expanded while maintaining his small, local bar vibe. This included building a half-wall with a tropical mural painted on the far wall of the newly acquired property, giving the illusion of coziness despite the increased space. The entire massive renovations—which included a dance floor with a retractable pool table, new bathrooms and new high tables and barstools—took less than five full days, thanks to a lot of help and planning. The larger Rick's Outer Bar reopened on July 4, 1989, with three hundred people waiting in line.

But even with the increased size, Rick's never lost its overall desire to be a local bar. There were no bouncers and no waitstaff, despite serving light food choices. This meant that it was up to the bartenders to engage every customer. It was obvious that Weeks truly cared about his customers, to the point that he would drive inebriated people home and back to their vehicles in the morning rather than letting them drive drunk.

Historic Bars, Clubs & Drinks

"That's how you run a local bar," Weeks explains. "You love your customers. I survived thirty years because of the locals when so many other bars came and went." It would be refreshed every few years with a new color scheme or memorabilia adorning the walls, but the heart and soul of Rick's Outer Bar remained. It would always be there, always open; in a fourteen-year stretch, the bar did not miss a single day. It was a place to drink and chat, to dance and sing—or to play darts, which became a large part of Rick's. Its Cape Cod Dart League, which began with itself along with the Chatham Squire, Spinnaker's in Harwich and Michael's Black Rose in Brewster, became so big that it included matches on television against some of the best in the world. The establishment increased its visibility throughout the Outer Cape with events like sailing contests and golf outings.

Business was great throughout the 1990s, but the smoking ban in bars of 2000 adversely affected Rick's. It was a hard few years, but Weeks persevered and began to get his head back above water. Sadly, the end of Rick's Outer Bar left a lot to be desired. First came a sharp increase in his rent by his new landlord, after which his lease was not extended. After thirty years of serving the locals, Rick Weeks took down his surfboards and photos and turned the lights off at his bar in 2011, but not by his own choice.

Now at seventy years old, Weeks still looks back fondly to his bar days, though he says that his love of surfing has been and always will be his life.

"Thirty years of being a rock and roll, party your ass off nightclub and nobody ever got hurt. We had a really good run and it was fun to be a part of." The surf legend still rides the waves, but it is stand-up paddle boarding that is his activity of choice. His next chapter includes a move to Portugal in the very near future. Today, the restaurant Local Break stands in the building where Rick Weeks built relationships with his loyal regulars and where those regulars built relationships with one another.

If one paid a visit to Rick's Outer Bar in its prime in the 1980s, one may have ordered an appropriate drink, the Surf and Sand Cocktail.

Cape Cod Nights

Surf and Sand Cocktail

1 ½ ounces brandy
½ ounce sweet vermouth
½ ounce Cherry Heering
2 ounces fresh orange juice
3 dashes cherry bitters
3 dashes Angostura bitters

Preparation: Add all of the ingredients to a shaker filled with ice. Shake, and strain into a chilled coupe or cocktail glass.

28.

SANDY POND CLUB

OLD TOWN BROOK ROAD, WEST YARMOUTH
1953–1978

It began its existence as a hunting lodge before becoming one of the legendary establishments during the golden age of Cape Cod nightlife. The Sandy Pond Club is still talked about glowingly by those who frequented it even thirty-five years after the building was burned down after the Town of Yarmouth bought the property.

The land on which the Sandy Pond Club once stood is at the north end of Town Brook Road in West Yarmouth. It was purchased in 1939 from Raymond Ellis by Nelson Cressy, Yarmouth's police chief, a position he had been promoted to the year previous. The property abutting Sandy Pond became home to a remote hunting lodge used by Chief Cressy. The lodge remained in his possession until 1953, when a future Cape Cod legend entered the picture.

Jack Braginton-Smith, who would gain fame decades later for his Jack's Outback restaurant on Route 6A in Yarmouth Port, showed his new wife, Dorothy, the site and Sandy Pond in 1953. She had come to the Cape from Rangely, Maine, after the death of her first husband, George Goodspeed, and the site gave her pleasant memories. She decided to purchase the land. Jack then took over Chief Cressy's lodge and turned it into the Sandy Pond Club. Popular establishments became a part of the family, as Braginton-Smith's father, Harold Smith, was the original owner of the nearby Mill Hill Club at the same time.

Though it would retain much of its hunting lodge charm, including a huge fireplace, Braginton-Smith had plans to make his new establishment one of a kind. Over time, he would purchase a total of ninety acres of land surrounding the club. The road leading to the Sandy Pond Club was dirt and filled with dangerous potholes. The potholes actually slowed people down as they drove the remote quarter-mile road, curbing any car accidents. The isolation of the road gave way to an oasis on the water, and patrons knew they had arrived. Despite the proximity of the new establishment, it quickly became an underground hit. Braginton-Smith incorporated the pond itself into the club by adding pontoon boats, a diving tower and a downstairs bar for those who chose to visit in swimsuits.

The Sandy Pond Club was nothing if not unique. It was a spot that had many distinctive traditions and activities that left an indelible mark on those who visited. There were oddities like the Lefty-Righty Club. This consisted of a cup hanging from either the left or right side of the club. On busy nights, folks would have to hold their drinks in the hand that corresponded to the mug. Throughout the night, a saxophone player at the club played a familiar tune, signaling that the cup was being moved and that all drinks had to be switched to the other hand. The music was a great cross-section, as there was rock 'n' roll in addition to some tremendous jazz legends, including Lou Colombo and Leroy Perkins's Excalibur Band, as well as famed pianist Bob Hayes. Dick Doherty of the equally legendary Crystal Palace in Hyannis played a jam session there in the days before he owned his own establishment. Iconic rock 'n' roll pioneer Chubby Checker even played a gig at the Sandy Pond Club. Jeans were not allowed; patrons dressed in a classy casual manner.

Braginton-Smith's son Brian lovingly refers to the Sandy Pond Club as "the original Jack's Outback, the old man at his best." Jack's Outback was another endeavor the elder Braginton-Smith owned, a beloved breakfast and lunch spot on Route 6A in Yarmouth Port.

Though Braginton-Smith sold the club in 1971, its popularity did not wane. It was leased by Cape Cod Happy Hour legend John Morgan, who ran it for three years as Groggery at Sandy Pond. On many nights, the club was packed wall to wall, with more than four hundred people squeezing inside. A season's pass cost only one dollar, and if one happened to be a year-round Cape Cod resident, one's pass was basically good "forever." It was a place locals and visitors as well as town firefighters and police frequented for the atmosphere as well as the cheap drinks. The beer of choice, Schlitz, cost fifty cents, while mixed drinks like the popular Cape Codder were seventy cents.

HISTORIC BARS, CLUBS & DRINKS

The site of the former Sandy Pond Club in West Yarmouth in 2018. *Courtesy of Christopher Setterlund.*

The 1970s was the heyday of raucous crowds at the Sandy Pond Club, but sadly, it did not last. After the 1978 season, the club closed due to financial difficulties, with the building remaining vacant for several years. By the early 1980s, the Town of Yarmouth had purchased the land, to eventually become a recreation area. The nearly seventy acres, including the hunting cabin turned roadhouse bar, cost the town $400,000 ($1.2 million in 2018). The Yarmouth Fire Department staged a controlled burn of the property on July 23, 1983, officially ending the club's reign in the woods near Sandy Pond.

The legacy of the Sandy Pond Club still lives on more than thirty-five years after its end. It lives on in the dirt road on which one can still drive and walk. It lives on in the shores of Sandy Pond, where former customers can relax and remember the good old days. It also lives on in the number of couples who met while working or patronizing the Sandy Pond Club. That may be its most enduring legacy: bringing people together.

In the heyday of the Sandy Pond Club, in the 1970s, a visitor not in the mood for a Cape Codder could try another popular drink of the era, a Tequila Sunrise.

Tequila Sunrise

2 ounces tequila
4 ounces orange juice
¼ ounce grenadine

Preparation: Add the tequila and then the orange juice to a chilled highball glass. Float the grenadine on top. Garnish it with an orange slice and a cherry.

29.
SMITH'S OLDE SURREY ROOM

704 Main Street, Falmouth
1946–1975

A truly unique nightclub and restaurant was born from a bowling alley in the year after World War II ended. The roots of the Surrey Room in Falmouth go back to the opening of the Falmouth Bowling Alley in 1939, and even further back than that to the days of the Revolutionary War.

The property on East Main Street in Falmouth that would one day house the Surrey Room began its existence at the forefront of something historical. Dr. Hugh G. Donaldson came to the United States from England during the Revolutionary War, settling in Falmouth. The doctor was one of the first to practice smallpox inoculation, enabling many to survive one of the deadliest diseases of the seventeenth and eighteenth centuries. After Donaldson died in 1812 at the age of fifty-five, his home remained in the family for another century. It was sold to Isaac Sabens, whose wife ran a laundry service out of the building just after World War I.

The second life of Dr. Donaldson's home would be the brainchild of Lester T. Crane. His idea was to turn the home into a bowling alley. After purchasing the property and beginning to do minor renovations to it, Crane petitioned the Town of Falmouth in March 1937 to allow him to build the bowling alley on the lot. It was approved shortly thereafter, and construction began on the 45-by-125-foot structure at a cost of approximately $6,100 ($108,000 in 2018). The Falmouth Bowling Alley debuted in November 1939 and was a success, with Crane himself partaking in leagues and

The interior of Smith's Surrey Room. *Courtesy of Mike Crew.*

tournaments held there. However, after a few years, Crane had another idea for the property, one that would bring even greater success.

As 1946 dawned, the local *Falmouth Enterprise* newspaper was inundated with advertisements featuring only images of question marks for weeks, piquing the interest of locals. During this time, big changes were happening to the Falmouth Bowling Alley. It came to a head on July 1, 1946, when Lester Crane's Surrey Room made its grand opening.

Hailed as an "unusual nightclub" at its debut, the Surrey Room bore little resemblance to the bowling alley that had resided there. The exterior had been adorned with hand-hewn shingles, bright red trim and light yellow window recesses. There was also a flagstone terrace covered with a portico. As to its name, the new establishment did indeed have surreys (a type of carriage popular in the late nineteenth and early twentieth centuries) placed in three corners of the room, fully equipped with seats for dining onboard. They were painstakingly purchased by Crane and his wife. Each surrey was painted black but for buttercup yellow wheels.

The year-round spot paid homage to its predecessor by including an addition on the front of the building called the Bowling Club Lounge. The pine-paneled lounge came with a U-shaped bar complete with a raised platform housing a piano for live music.

The opening event at the Surrey Room was a private dinner-dance sponsored by the World War II veterans of Falmouth. It included an orchestra and a quartet and was attended by more than 150 people. The public opening was a few days later, on July 4. Lester Crane promoted his new establishment as a nightclub devoted to dinner and dancing with a menu of freshly cooked luxuries like lobster and steak dinners. It created an authentic atmosphere of the era of the surrey.

The attention to detail by Crane worked, as the Surrey Room, which could seat three hundred, routinely squeezed more than four hundred inside for events. The initial season was a rousing success. In subsequent years, it would become popular for weddings in addition to more private events. Though it was successful, Lester Crane sold the Surrey Room in January 1950 to Daniel Smith. Crane left Cape Cod for Sarasota, Florida, after the sale, continuing in the restaurant industry. Daniel Smith immediately began to make changes to the popular nightspot.

Smith began by adding a 40-by-45-foot extension to the front of the club at a cost of $20,000 ($213,000 in 2018). He then increased the parking area, allowing for up to two hundred cars. Smith brought a relatively new luxury, the television, to his Surrey Room. He completed the improvements by hiring Daniel Bartolomei to be his executive chef. Bartolomei would gain further fame locally when he opened Danny-Kay's a few years later.

The new Smith's Olde Surrey Room began to move away from Lester Crane's initial vision when Smith removed the actual surreys from the interior in May 1951. Despite a thorough renovation of the establishment's interior, Smith maintained the Surrey Room name. He created his own beloved traditions, including an annual venison dinner each January that filled the Surrey Room to its maximum.

Trouble came for the Surrey Room in December 1954, when owner Daniel Smith was found guilty of tax evasion and sentenced to two years in prison. He was allowed to run the operations of the business through New Year's before reporting to the federal correctional institute in Danbury, Connecticut. The day-to-day operations would be run in his absence by Smith's wife.

Despite his incarceration, Smith's nightspot remained popular throughout the 1950s. Upon his release, a second addition was built on the Surrey Room, at forty-five feet by forty-five feet, in 1958. The 1960s began with sad news, as Surrey Room founder Lester Crane died on June 25, 1960, at the age of sixty-four. However, its deeper foray into food service paid off when, in 1961, the Surrey Room was featured in the prestigious

Adventures in Good Eating, published by Duncan Hines. At the time, the publication showcased only 9,200 eating and lodging establishments out of more than 500,000 in the country. The nightspot held on to its appeal with routine jazz events and after-dinner dancing, which had become rare.

Daniel Smith sold the Surrey Room in the mid-1970s. It was purchased by Dr. Stanley Watson, a microbiologist at Woods Hole Oceanographic Institute. He briefly used it as headquarters for Associates of Cape Cod, a real estate and biotech company that would move to the Falmouth Technology Park. As of 2018, the site of Lester Crane's and Daniel Smith's Surrey Room is affordable housing apartments.

Those who frequented the Surrey Room in its heyday in the 1950s may have enjoyed a drink called a Singapore Sling. Here is how to make one.

Singapore Sling

¾ ounce gin
¼ ounce Grand Marnier
¼ ounce cherry liqueur
¼ ounce herbal liqueur
1 ounce pineapple juice
½ ounce fresh lime juice
1 dash bitters
club soda to top

Preparation: Add all of the ingredients except the club soda into a shaker with ice and shake. Strain into a highball glass and top with the club soda. Garnish it with an orange slice and a cherry.

30.
SOUTHWARD INN

107 Main Street/30 Route 28, Orleans
1916–1971

It began during wartime and changed locations early in its existence. Either of those could have easily spelled doom for the Southward Inn. However, not only did it survive, it also thrived for more than four decades. It would go on to become the place to be for entertainment in Orleans in the middle of the twentieth century.

The story of the Southward Inn begins in 1916 and does include a man whose last name is Southward. George Southward purchased property in Orleans owned by Edgar Snow in May and created the first Southward Inn along with his wife, Rebecca, on Main Street. The establishment barely had time to get its name out there when the United States entered World War I in 1917. Two years later, Southward took a risk on moving his fledgling business to a different location.

At the intersection of present-day Route 28 and Cove Road once stood the Newcomb Lodge. In the early twentieth century, it was built as the home of Alexander Newcomb. He was a well-known businessman in Orleans, holding positions such as bank president, town clerk and selectman for eighteen years. Newcomb was believed to be the first person to own an automobile in the town. Unfortunately, he also became the first person to die in an automobile accident in town as well, in May 1911. His home was left to his adopted daughter Mary, who turned it into the Newcomb Lodge.

A postcard of the Southward Inn from the 1940s. *Courtesy of Sturgis Library.*

She sold it to James Eldredge in 1917, who in turn sold it to Southward in February 1919. It was a move of only half a mile, but it eventually took Southward Inn light years from where it began.

Southward Inn was a fully functioning restaurant as well as a hotel, picking up steam in popularity in the Roaring Twenties. By the time 1925 rolled around, George Southward was sixty-one years old and looking to reduce his workload. He sold his establishment to Camille Remillard. Unfortunately, that marriage did not last long. In 1932, Southward Inn was back on the market. With no other offers, George bought back the inn, reassuming management duties.

Southward again relinquished control of his establishment in 1935. Bill and Eve Rich took over and began to push the inn to new heights. Southward's wife, Rebecca, died the next year; George passed in 1938, closing the book on the original owners.

As the 1930s ended and the 1940s began, business at the Southward Inn continued to grow. The Riches kept the beautiful ambience of the inn with the warm fireplace at the entrance. They added the special touch of a loudmouthed parrot who enjoying chatting it up with patrons, a unique sight for a Cape Cod establishment. Folk artist, entrepreneur and local celebrity Peter Hunt added the finishing touches to the grand masterpiece that was the Southward Inn.

Historic Bars, Clubs & Drinks

Hunt's furnishing designs gained great acclaim in outlets such as *Life* and *Mademoiselle* magazines. He opened a collection of shops in Provincetown along Commercial Street known as Peasant Village, establishing his style and legend on the Cape in the 1930s and 1940s. In 1951, Hunt designed the Carriage Room at Southward Inn. Furnished with antiques, copperware, old photos and coach lamps, it was a perfect capper to the inn. In 1954, Hunt wrote his *Cape Cod Cookbook*, using recipes from Southward Inn, forever preserving its legacy.

It was after the debut of the Carriage Room that the entertainment at Southward Inn really took off. Under the ownership of Frank and Betty Richards, who purchased it in 1952, the Orleans staple began to bring in some of the most noted jazz artists of the decade. Pianist Dick Miller and Leroy "Sam" Parkins and the Excalibur Jazz Band, as well as others, thrilled audiences with their slick style. The Southward Inn gained notoriety quickly as an entertainment scene, so much so that popular New York jazz pianist Bud Blacklock added it to his list of club acts along with other Cape favorites like the Atlantic House. In addition to that impressive list, square dancing became a craze at Southward Inn, to the point that every Friday night, Fred Moynahan and his orchestra would perform for those wishing to show off their dancing skills.

From jazz music to square dancing, from the Carriage Room to other unique lounges like the Garden Room, Fisherman's Bar and Terrace Lounge, the Southward Inn had numerous reasons why it was so popular for weddings, private functions and birthdays. Small touches like the chatty parrot, the king and queen playing cards on the restroom doors and even the beautiful dogwood tree that attracted attention each year when it was in bloom made this spot unlike any other on the Cape. However, its sale to Delbert Johnson, then owner of the Governor Prence Motor Lodge in North Truro, in 1961, for $125,000 ($1 million in 2018), proved to be the beginning of the end.

In April 1962, after massive interior renovations, the Southward Inn was rechristened the Nauset Inn. It was not

A Manhattan cocktail. *Courtesy of Graeme Maclean.*

associated with a previous establishment in Orleans that went by the same name in the 1920s. Despite focusing more on the nightlife aspect, the business lasted a few years before falling back to the Southward Inn name. The constant changes cost the establishment its loyal local following, and it was put up for auction in 1971. It was bought by Richard Harris, who rechristened it the Olde Inn. It was closed by the board of health in 1974, never to reopen. The wrecking ball ended the Southward Inn's reign on May 10, 1977.

As of 2018, the Masonic Lodge stands on the site of the original Southward Inn on Main Street; a Bank of America stands at the site of the second Southward Inn on Route 28.

Those who frequented the Southward Inn in its heyday in the 1950s and early 1960s may have had the chance to enjoy a Manhattan.

Manhattan

2 ounces rye whiskey
1 ounce sweet vermouth
5 drops Angostura bitters

Preparation: Mix all of the ingredients and serve in a cocktail glass with ice. Garnish with a cherry.

31.
STORYVILLE

Route 124, Pleasant Lake, Harwich
1957–1961

Cape Cod and jazz—the two go together like peanut butter and jelly. The beautiful peninsula and the popular music genre have been connected throughout the twentieth and twenty-first centuries. The Columns in West Dennis was well known for its jazz in its 1970s heyday. However, there was a spot that rivaled it as far as sheer talent appearing there. For a few brief years in the middle of the twentieth century, one place shined brighter than all the others when it came to Cape Cod jazz, and that was Storyville in Harwich.

Storyville may have opened its doors along Pleasant Lake in Harwich in 1957, but its legacy goes back much further, to the waning years of the nineteenth century. In 1897, the original Storyville was opened in New Orleans, Louisiana. As jazz was in its infancy, a district of the city was created by Alderman Sidney Story to house the new music. Years later, accomplished musician George Wein opened his own Storyville in Boston. Wein, who would gain fame for creating the Newport Jazz Festival and Newport Folk Festival, made it his mission to bring the most talented jazz artists to play at his Boston locale. With his success at Storyville-Boston secure, Wein planned his next step.

In 1956, Wein spent the summer in Wellfleet, playing music at local nightspots with his close friend Paul Nossiter. It was during this time that

A Storyville menu cover. *Courtesy of Doug Walker.*

he fell in love with Cape Cod and decided that it needed a permanent spot to showcase jazz. He found a perfect spot in a former Cape restaurant. The Robin Hood Inn gained fame in the 1920s as a Prohibition-era spot built atop the filled-in remains of the Cape's first cranberry bog, owned by Cyrus Cahoon and designed by his cousin Alvan.

Wein purchased the former restaurant turned inn the following year. Although he added a wing to the home to bring its capacity from three hundred up to six hundred people, he kept much of its medieval interior charm. Storyville-Harwich set the tone for its all too brief existence on its very first night. It was on July 4, 1957, that the Cape's hottest jazz club debuted with none other than Louis Armstrong playing two long sets to a raucous crowd. The opening season would see other legends of the day, such as Dave Brubeck and Erroll Garner, stopping in to ply their trade for weeklong engagements. The first season at Storyville was a huge success, a harbinger of things to come.

Initially, the establishment served only drinks to its patrons. However, with the rousing success of the opening season, Wein decided to serve food as well, hiring a chef and maître d'. Opening night saw throngs of people waiting three hours for their dinners, as Wein and Nossiter were not restaurateurs. Though they had the "hippest menu," complete with steaks, ribs, chicken, lobster and more, the foray into serving food lasted only a month. They served high-quality food at reasonable prices, losing money on the venture.

Despite that failure, the musical acts continued to be what drew the people. Stars like Ella Fitzgerald, Duke Ellington, Pee Wee Russell, Benny Goodman, Sarah Vaughan and others made the trip over the Cape Cod Canal to the woods of rural Harwich to entertain the masses during the ten-week summer season. But the supernova that was Storyville could not be sustained.

In 1959, the star power was still there, with mainstays like Armstrong, Vaughan, Garner and others returning. But it was a double-edged sword. In order to bring in such acts, they needed to be paid, yet there was only so much that Wein and Nossiter could charge people to get into Storyville. This meant that the club was not making much, if anything, in terms of profit. It was around this time that George Wein began being stretched too thin with his commitments to the Newport Jazz Festival, Newport Folk Festival and other projects. He simply could not devote as much time and energy to his Harwich spot.

In 1960, the star power of the musical acts waned. As the big names of jazz began to get nationwide exposure, Storyville was not able to afford to bring them in to play. Customers had been accustomed to the big names, and when they became less frequent, the business went as well. Wein first closed his Boston Storyville location after the 1960 season, leaving Harwich to run for one more season.

Despite the impending end of the establishment, the 1961 season still managed to attract megastars like Duke Ellington, Erroll Garner and Louis Armstrong. However, the death knell for Storyville came when the wildly popular Kingston Trio failed to sell enough tickets for a show. The rising cost for acts and ticket prices was a combination too powerful for Wein and Nossiter to overcome. Storyville was shuttered after the 1961 season. The building itself would have another chapter. After being sold to Joel Schiavone, it was renamed the Red Garter. The name was again changed, to Your Father's Mustache, due to a copyright problem. The establishment burned down later in the 1960s. Your Father's Mustache was reopened in Dennis Port on the first floor of an old barn. The upstairs space became known as the Improper Bostonian, which still operates as of 2018. Storyville is now nothing more than a short blip on the radar, with no physical remains of its existence, leaving nothing behind but its legacy of great jazz music.

Those who frequented Storyville during its brief run may have been served a Blue Hawaiian.

Blue Hawaiian

1 ounce light rum
2 ounces pineapple juice
1 ounce blue curacao liqueur
1 ounce cream of coconut

Preparation: Pour ingredients into shaker with ice. Shake well and strain into a glass. Garnish it with a pineapple slice and a cherry.

32.
VELVET HAMMER / RED DOOR / BACKSIDE SALOON

209 Main Street, Hyannis
1970–1983

In the history of Cape Cod nightlife, there have been many buildings that have held more than one establishment. It is common for one place to close and be replaced by another of the same ilk. What is much less common, very rare in fact, is for there to be more than one popular establishment located under the same roof at the same time. For several years in Dennis Port, this was the case when Improper Bostonian and Your Father's Mustache operated inside the same historic old barn. However, for a time in downtown Hyannis, there was one spot that housed not one, not two, but three different popular nightspots under one roof. This is the story of the Velvet Hammer, Red Door and Backside Saloon.

The Velvet Hammer was originally the property of Leonard Healy, who also owned Deacon's Perch in Yarmouth Port, when it was opened in 1970. Before becoming a well-known entertainment complex, the building at 209 Main Street housed Coleman's Park Square Market, the Hyannis Inn and Porthole Lounge at different times. Initially, the Velvet Hammer carried the name Velvet Hammer Inn and was seen as a Top 40 club where the ladies went, so the men followed. It at first held special lavish parties, such as New Year's galas, with lobster and champagne. But as the years passed, events like those became common at the rear entrance known as the Backside Saloon. The complex also included the Red Door, which served drinks and food in addition to showing movies. It was also joined

The Hyannis Inn, predecessor to the Velvet Hammer, in the late 1950s. *Courtesy of Sturgis Library.*

by the laundry room of the neighboring Eastender Motel, which Healy bought and converted into the Expansion Room. This became connected to the Backside along with the Cafe Ritz.

Healy's tenure as owner of Velvet Hammer saw some big-name musical talent working the stage, including Buddy Rich, The Platters, The Drifters and the Kingston Trio in 1971 alone. The "Hammer" attracted the college-age crew, even with its strict dress code of no jeans. It bucked the trend of disco music in the 1970s by diving headlong into jazz, with Cape luminaries like Lou Colombo and Dave McKenna frequenting the Hammer's stage. It was the place to "dance, listen, shoot the breeze, and feel nice," as advertisements from the time said.

The Velvet Hammer complex enjoyed great success in the early to mid-1970s with its varied selection of entertainment all under one roof. It truly had something for every person and every age group. But despite the ample crowds paying covers at times to see the great musical acts, money problems were growing for Healy. The cost of running the operation was outweighing the profits gained. By 1978, he was looking to sell the entire property.

A buyer arose in the form of Corydon Litchard, former owner of the Mill Hill Club in West Yarmouth. He, along with partner Chris Patterson, purchased the entire complex from Healy in early 1979, assuming all of the debts owed to creditors. Healy moved on and failed in a bid for the former Penn Central Railroad property in downtown Hyannis in 1979. That property would later be purchased by John Morgan and become Pufferbellies.

The new owners kept Velvet Hammer and Backside Saloon essentially intact, although the Hammer embraced a Top 40 music atmosphere and Backside catered to the older crowd. They worked on revamping the Red Door, which had seen changes in style several times over the years, from jazz to nightclub to lunch restaurant. The Velvet Hammer complex reopened in March 1979 under the new ownership.

The reopening of the complex was met with huge success again, and the years 1979–81 were a return to the norm for the Velvet Hammer. There were lines out the door regularly on both side of the complex. Despite this, the debt that Litchard had assumed was simply too much, and the company remained in the red. In November 1981, after business had dipped during the summer Litchard filed for bankruptcy. Late in the summer of 1982, the establishment was prepared to go up for sale at auction.

The Velvet Hammer for all intents and purposes was closed as it awaited sale from late 1982 into early 1983. Litchard was attempting to organize a new group to purchase it outright. In February 1984, the complex was again sold, this time to Stephen Jones, who leased the Backside Saloon to Charles Leonard, owner of two other Hyannis establishments, M.D. Armstrong's and East End Pub. Leonard reopened Backside shorty thereafter as a light food restaurant with a small bar and no live entertainment and gave it a final lease on life for a few years. However, the Velvet Hammer's lights never came back on. It was eventually repurposed as retail space.

More than thirty years have passed since the Velvet Hammer was closed. Although the Backside Saloon lasted for a few more years, the complex lost much of its luster when the Hammer ceased to be. Today, people still remember fondly when passing by the old building that remains standing at the east end of Main Street. It houses businesses such as a nail salon. But it houses something even greater inside its walls: the memories of the golden age of Cape Cod's nightlife.

If one paid a visit to any of the three arms of the entertainment complex during its heyday in the 1970s, one may have ordered a popular drink of the time, a Scarlett O'Hara

Cape Cod Nights

Scarlett O'Hara

2 ounces Southern Comfort
dash of fresh lime juice
6 ounces cranberry juice

Preparation: Mix all of the ingredients with cracked ice in a shaker and strain into a glass. Garnish with a lime wedge.

33.
WINDJAMMER

380 BARNSTABLE ROAD, HYANNIS
1964–2005

Cape Cod has a deep connection to the sea, as it is surrounded by it on all sides, thanks to the creation of the Cape Cod Canal. To those who enjoy escapes onto the salty waves, the term *windjammer* likely brings to mind a large merchant sailing ship built for carrying cargo. However, to those who grew up on the Cape in the latter half of the twentieth century, the term likely brings to mind the highly popular bar that resided within eyesight of the Barnstable Airport.

The story of Cape Cod's most famous windjammer, the lounge that bore the name, began in 1964. It was the brainchild of Frederick "Bud" McClane, who would end up with his handprints all over two other legendary Barnstable establishments, Mitchell's Steak House and the Mattakeese Wharf. McClane partnered with Stretch Hinckley to run the new lounge. It was initially referred to as the Windjammer Lounge Club, as laws of the day did not allow bars to be open on Sundays. Membership was free. The lounge opened seasonally beginning on April 1, with lines of returning customers waiting outside. In time, it would eventually become a year-round business. McClane's establishment would be known in the 1960s as much for its menu as for anything else. The Windjammer's beloved options included its French onion soup, prime rib, reubens and Ivans. In fact, its overstuffed sandwiches were extremely popular, especially during a time when such things were not the norm.

As the 1960s drew to a close, the Windjammer saw its focus begin to shift with the arrival of one of Cape Cod's most beloved entertainers. Beginning in 1966, Cape Cod's "First Lady of Jazz," Marie Marcus, made the stage at the Windjammer the main home for her and her band through 1970. It made the establishment more than simply a restaurant; it became a destination for great entertainment.

As time passed, the upstairs part of the Windjammer remained a fixture for the great food served there, becoming known as the Galley, while the downstairs level became the bar. Its pool tables became so popular that the Barnstable police would come in to play on their days off. There was also a special seating section called the "Senators Corner," complete with a quarter board with that name. At times during the 1970s, the Windjammer Lounge had up to 80 percent of its sales coming from alcohol. The imprint left by Marie Marcus brought countless other great local and regional entertainers to the stage, in turn leading to more drinking during the Cape's golden age of nightlife.

Bud McClane saw much of the Windjammer's success, but he would have to sell his part in the popular establishment after suffering a stroke. In 1976, the business was purchased by Peter Feeney, a retired Barnstable School District English teacher, and Ed Kennedy. Feeney became a hugely popular fixture, regularly mingling with the crowds at the Windjammer. In 1978, he branched out the Jammer by winning the right to the concessions at the crowded Kalmus Beach in Hyannis. Feeney also had a hand in the ban of local liquor license quotas in Barnstable in 1978 after fighting in court as a result of being initially refused a new liquor license after purchasing the Windjammer in 1976. He won that fight, but another battle with the town would not go his way.

It was smooth sailing for the Windjammer throughout the 1980s and 1990s, with the downstairs lounge cleaning up with its live entertainment while the Galley held its own serving delicious food upstairs. There was even a Windjammer Triathlon race held beginning in 1982, with three hundred participants. It was renamed the Seaside Triathlon in 1984.

In 2000, the town of Barnstable banned smoking indoors at bars and restaurants. This ruling hurt the business at the Windjammer, though the keno game and pool tables helped to soften the downfall at first. The sales of food at the Galley picked up after the smoking ban. Despite that bit of good news, overall, it was a downward trend. Feeney fought the ban for more than a year before it was upheld.

The trend continued for the longtime Hyannis establishment. Feeney tried to swim upstream, petitioning in 2003 to take "Lounge" from the

Historic Bars, Clubs & Drinks

Windjammer's name in order to make a transition from the bar-first reputation and to an emphasis on the restaurant. He said that by 2003 alcohol made up only 20 percent of sales, compared to 80 percent in its heyday. Another problem the Windjammer faced was the incessant traffic from the Airport Rotary. Feeney saw it as a deterrent to potential customers. It had contributed to the departure of the Chili's restaurant located on the rotary in 2005. The very same year, Feeney sold his stake in the Windjammer to Rick Angelini.

Despite the good intentions of trying to revamp the Windjammer as the Wianno Grille, an "upscale sports bar," the new ownership failed to supply the necessary license and permits, causing it to take a year for the name to be changed. The new establishment lasted until 2011 before being replaced by McGrath's Saloon, which still stands as of 2018.

If one had visited the Windjammer Lounge to see Marie Marcus in her tenure in the late 1960s, one may have ordered a drink like a Planter's Punch.

Planter's Punch

3 ounces dark rum
¾ ounce fresh lime juice
1 ounce simple syrup
1 bar spoon Grenadine
3 dashes Angostura bitters
1 splash soda water

Preparation: Add all of the ingredients into a shaker with ice, and shake vigorously. Strain into a collins glass over crushed ice. Top with a splash of soda water. Garnish with a mint sprig.

34.
ZACK'S LOUNGE

146 Sandwich Road, East Falmouth
1950–1978

Cape Cod in the twentieth century had numerous legendary nightspots. They dotted the landscape in the well-populated areas like Hyannis, Provincetown and Falmouth. However, there was one place that received recognition on a national level. It was a place located far from the relative bright lights of Falmouth and Hyannis. It was a place located in the small town of Mashpee. It was Zack's Place, and according to *Time* magazine, it was the "original real swinging nightclub on Cape."

The story of Zack's begins with the immigration to America from Fogo, Cape Verde, of young Zachary Roderick in 1907, when he was seventeen. Almost immediately, Roderick found himself in the business world, working hard at jobs in a grocery store on Trotting Park Road in Falmouth, as a fruit seller and as a taxi driver. But there was a different path he wished to take. In 1946, Roderick first attempted to get into the liquor sales business legally by requesting a seasonal liquor license for a new package store. During Prohibition, he had actually been busted in a liquor raid in 1924 for possession of a gallon of moonshine, though there is no record of any fine or punishment for the infraction. His request for a seasonal liquor license in 1946 was rejected. He vigorously appealed it, and the license was granted the following year.

Historic Bars, Clubs & Drinks

Zack's Lounge in the late 1960s. *Courtesy of Mike Crew.*

Roderick's seasonal package store on Sandwich Road in the village of Teaticket became a success, allowing him to take the next step in his business journey. By a stroke of luck, a new, larger building became available where he could move his package store. In July 1948, the Boa Venture Club, also on Sandwich Road, had been foreclosed upon by Wareham Savings Bank. The building and approximately one acre of land were bought at auction by Roderick, and he moved his business inside its walls.

In 1949, Roderick sold his seasonal liquor license at a cost of $10,000 ($105,000 in 2018) to Lawrence Antonellis. This did not mean Roderick was getting out of the liquor business, though. He in turn applied for a license to sell alcohol in his building, but to run it as a nightclub and bar. In June 1950, the license was granted. Zachary Roderick opened his new establishment and called it Zack's Place.

Before the end of its first summer in business, though, Zack's Place came under fire from locals in the area, mainly the family living next door to the property. Arguments were made that Roderick's business was operating in a residential zone and that the establishment's license should have been given to a business that operated as a restaurant. There were claims of noise and rowdiness, fights and an increase in vehicles, posing a danger to children. The vast majority of the complaints were dismissed, as countless patrons of the popular new establishment came forward to speak of how well it was run by Roderick. This helped him win his suit. In June 1951, he was denied a club license because he was properly incorporated. He applied for and received a restaurant permit the following month.

He moved Zack's Place a little way down Sandwich Road into the business district in 1953 near the Cape Verdean Club. Business ran smoothly from then on for Zachary Roderick, until his death at age sixty-seven on December 29, 1957. His son Charles took the reins of the establishment from there.

After Charles took over the establishment, Zack's truly hit its stride as a place to be and to be seen on the Upper Cape. The increased popularity led

Charles Roderick to seek out a year-round liquor license; until then, Zack's had only been seasonal. The license was denied. Roderick vehemently protested, claiming that Zack's was the only African American–friendly bar in the area—when the season ended, his patrons would have to travel as far away as New Bedford to be served. Unfortunately, the appeal was denied. Roderick made the best of what he had. It would prove to be more than good enough.

In 1966, *Time* gave Zack's its greatest publicity by mentioning it in an issue, calling it, among other things, "the place to go on the Cape." Charles Roderick brought in big-name musical acts to grace his establishment, including The Commodores, Bo Diddley, Fabulous Farquahr, The Platters and Tavares, among others. Roderick remained friends with Lionel Richie and the Tavares brothers for the rest of his life. Around this same time, the club's name was changed to Zack's Lounge. The increased visibility from the *Time* article, advertising in Boston and the popular musical acts allowed Charles to open a sister Zack's in Boston, along with the Lion in Falmouth.

When man walked on the moon on July 20, 1969, the legendary Dick Doherty, that night's entertainment, led a conga line out of the club and across Sandwich Road. Guitar players, dancers, average partygoers and even Little Richard swung from the rafters over the dance floor at Zack's. There was rarely an empty parking spot. Charles Roderick catered to countless locals and visitors before finally selling the club in 1978. It was renamed R.C.'s Lounge, owned by Ralph Castellano, before ultimately burning to the ground suspiciously in the early 1980s. As of 2018, Papa Jake's Pizza stands on the property where Zack's Lounge once stood.

The huge success of Zack's Lounge and Charles Roderick in the 1960s and 1970s have cemented both as undeniable icons of the Cape Cod nightlife scene. It is assured that there will never be another club like Zack's or another owner like Charles.

Although Zack's routinely sold more beer than nearly any club in the east, if one paid a visit there at its peak in the late 1960s, one could have ordered the popular mixed drink the Gimlet.

Gimlet

2½ ounces gin
½ ounce fresh lime juice
½ ounce simple syrup

Preparation: Add all of the ingredients into a shaker with ice and shake. Strain into a chilled cocktail glass or an old-fashioned glass filled with fresh ice. Garnish with a lime wheel.

NOTE

All of the facts and information in this book were gathered through countless hours of research using newspaper and magazine archives, along with personal interviews with numerous former owners, employees and patrons of the nightclubs, bars and other establishments included. They are accurate to the best of the author's ability.

BIBLIOGRAPHY

Active Paper Archive. *Falmouth Enterprise.* http://www.digital.olivesoftware.com/Olive/APA/Falmouth/#panel=home.

———. Sturgis Library's *Barnstable Patriot* Digital Newspaper Archive. digital.olivesoftware.com/Olive/APA/Sturgis/default.aspx#panel=home.

Crosby, Johanna. "A Trip in Time with the Panama Club." *Cape Cod Times*, January 7, 2011. www.capecodtimes.com/article/20060710/news01/307109969.

Dennis Historical Society. Accessed October 17, 2018. http://www.dennishistsoc.org.

Digital Commonwealth. https://www.digitalcommonwealth.org.

Dunlap, David W. Building Provincetown. http://www.buildingprovincetown.wordpress.com.

Eldredge Library Online Database. eldredge.microsearch.net/Home.

Historical Newspapers, 1700s–2000s. Retrieved October 17, 2018. https://www.newspapers.com.

Internet Archive. https://archive.org.

Liquor.com. March 9, 2017. www.liquor.com.

NewspaperArchive. Retrieved November 22, 2018. https://newspaperarchive.com.

Pratt, David. "Pufferbellies Hopes Transportation Center Will Drive in Biz." *Barnstable Patriot*, March 3, 2001. www.barnstablepatriot.com/home2/index.php/option=com_content/task=view/id=126/Itemid=33.

Bibliography

Provincetown Advocate Online Newspaper Archives. http://www.advocate.provincetown-ma.gov.

Provincetown History Preservation Project. www.provincetownhistoryproject.com.

Town of Mashpee Documents Archive. Retrieved November 15, 2018. http://records.mashpeema.gov.

Town of Orleans. *Cape Codder* Online Archives. https://www.town.orleans.ma.us/snow-library/pages/special-collections.

Your Father's Mustache Band. www.mustacheband.com/index.html.

ABOUT THE AUTHOR

Christopher Setterlund is a twelfth-generation Cape Codder whose roots go back to the second *Mayflower* voyage. He is the author of *Historic Restaurants of Cape Cod* (The History Press, 2017). He is also the author of three books in the *In My Footsteps* travel book series, which features Cape Cod, Martha's Vineyard and Nantucket. In addition to books, the author has contributed work to the Cape Cod Chamber of Commerce, *Cape Cod Life* magazine, *Cape Cod* magazine, CapeCod.com and the Travel Channel. Away from writing, he has been a WITS-certified personal trainer since 2015. He enjoys running and photography and is a lover of travel.

www.ingramcontent.com/pod-product-compliance
Lightning Source LLC
Chambersburg PA
CBHW042140160426
43201CB00021B/2350